OUT OF ASHES

Helen Wells Quintela

Foreword by John Perkins

HERALD PRESS
Scottdale, Pennsylvania
Waterloo, Ontario

Library of Congress Cataloging-in-Publication Data
Quintela, Helen Wells, 1953-
    Out of ashes / Helen Wells Quintela ; foreword by José Ortiz.
       p. cm.
    Includes bibliographical references.
    ISBN 0-8361-3554-7 (alk. paper)
    1. Quintela, Helen Wells, 1953-   . 2. Quintela, Alberto. 3. St.
Paul Mennonite Fellowship (Saint Paul, Minn.)—History.
4. Mennonites—Minnesota—Biography. I. Title.
BX8143.Q55A3   1991
289.7'092'2—dc20
[B]   91-10447
                                            CIP

The paper used in this publication is recycled and meets the minimum requirements of American National Standard for Information Sciences—Permanence of Paper for Printed Library Materials, ANSI Z39.48-1984.

Scripture quotations are from the *Holy Bible: New International Version*. Copyright © 1973, 1978, 1984 International Bible Society. Used by permission of Zondervan Bible Publishers.

To Alberto

Blessed is the man
who does not walk in the counsel of the
        wicked. . . .
He is like a tree planted by streams of water,
which yields its fruit in season
and whose leaf does not wither.

Psalm 1

Blessed are you, my husband.
May you live to see your children's children.

FOREWORD

Helen Quintela's book *Out of Ashes* needs to be read by everyone who is involved in urban ministry or who sees the plight of our urban communities and is looking for creative solutions to the problems we are facing. Helen's experience in her community accurately reflects the pain and joy that urban community development is all about. Living in the community with the Robinson family, Helen was exposed to and received the pain, the agony, and the sense of inferiority that were in that family.

As a partner in an interracial marriage, Helen bore even more guilt and pain. Because of her privileged background and race, she was not the target of the hostilities Alberto endured. Yet he is her husband, and his pain is her pain. The pain, I know, was great because I experienced some of the same pain Alberto experienced, ulcers and all.

Helen and Alberto were not prepared to handle the pain of racism and hatred. None of us ever are. Yet they made a response. Helen and Alberto's desire for reconciliation, in the midst of that painful and scarring experience, is a testament to their faith in Christ and to the presence of their Mennonite fellowship in the community. The gospel reconciles people to God and to each other across racial, social, and economic barriers. Reconciliation, the very work of the gospel, exemplified in Jesus' agonizing death on the cross, cannot take place without pain.

Throughout their relationship with the Robinsons they did their best to seek a peaceful resolution. When time for action came, they sought the good of the Robinsons as well as their own. As their spirits and bodies wasted away they nevertheless stuck firm to the principles of their faith. With the love and support of their church members they were able to propose and carry out plans for mediation and resolution, all the while continuing to contribute to the community, Alberto with his legal skills, Helen with her teaching skills. The church was the family that they leaned on in a difficult time.

With Helen as its pastor, the St. Paul Mennonite Fellowship is today doubly blessed: she exemplifies in her life the shepherding servant that a pastor should be. And she is an experienced soldier in the battle for our urban communities. Her fellowship would not be so enriched if it had not been for the suffering and the pain that she and Alberto went through. Living among the people in the community of need made their life and faith real and meaningful.

> —*Dr. John Perkins, President*
> *John M. Perkins Foundation for*
> *Reconciliation and Development*
> *Pasadena, California*

AUTHOR'S PREFACE

I am haunted by fire and smoke. It doesn't matter where I am, what I am doing. The smell of it makes me fight rising internal panic. I must locate the fire; I must be sure it isn't consuming something or someone.

Because of my fear, I struggle to contemplate the image of God speaking out of a burning bush. I still seek to embrace the imagery of the Holy Spirit coming as tongues of fire in Acts 2. My fear can be a wall between me and these compelling images of my God.

In these past nine years, I have received some healing of these fears. They are with me still, but their power to undo me and build walls between me and God is greatly diminished.

One source of healing was the Monday morning prayer ceremony at Red School House, an alternative school in St. Paul, Minnesota, founded and directed by Native American peoples. In the year that I taught there, I learned to respect again the power and the spirit of fire. I learned that there are two fires: a fire that consumes and a fire that purifies and releases.

In our culture, we respect only the fire that consumes; we use fire to consume the earth's resources and to burn that for which we have no use. We have much to learn about the fire that releases and purifies.

God appeared to Moses in the burning bush, but the bush was not burned up. The flame of the Holy Spirit came upon the followers of Jesus at Pentecost, but did not burn their hair. Later, the flames of this world would consume their bodies. But the Holy Spirit bears witness to their continuing presence in our lives as clouds of witnesses around us. Their faith could not be burned up. It lives to this day.

I pray that this story will be a testimony to the Holy Flame that burns even in the darkest night of our lives. If it is the story of an earthly fire that consumed hope and love, it is also a witness to the heavenly fire which released a people of faith from ashes.

● ● ●

This book was written originally as a Senior Honor's Project during my final term (spring, 1990) at United Theological Seminary, New Brighton, Minnesota. I gratefully acknowledge the theological community which gave me time and support to reflect on and tell of an experience that so deeply changed me.

I particularly thank Henry Gustafson, then professor of New Testament Theology, my adviser and mentor for this project. Those drawn to the edge of their seats in his classroom know that when Henry speaks, he weaves a tapestry of wisdom and conviction.

Mary Potter Engel's Constructive Theology class brought me to the threshold of the room in which I had locked this story.

Helen Archibald, my faculty adviser, encouraged me throughout my seminary sojourn.

Professor Don White shared his understanding of the Anabaptist tradition.

I thank them, and all the many persons who helped me find my distinctive voice in the ecumenical community that is United Seminary.

The names of persons in an adversarial relationship to us or in our Baker Street neighborhood have been changed. I pray that the story is justly and truthfully told, and that we all recognize ourselves in both the worst and the best of its human struggles.

I extend my gratitude to both family and friends, some of whom, since this story took place, have joined the great cloud of witnesses that surround us.

To my dear mother, I would like to say a very inadequate thank you. She and I remember the little girl who would not speak and who later struggled to master the written word. If I speak now, it is because the two of us set sail together in the old cherry rocker to the tune of endless songs and rhymes that she supplied each night for our journey.

And if I have been able to weave words into a story of pain and redemption, it is because she taught me at the loom of poetry which she somehow found time to compose. Being a woman of the Word, she laid the foundation for this book.

—*Helen Wells Quintela*
St. Paul, Minnesota

1

Alberto and I started our married life much like any young couple, full of hope and joy. We were married on August 7, 1976, in a small church wedding in my hometown of Greenville, South Carolina. We had met at Harvard University Graduate School of Education the year before, where we were both working on M.Ed. degrees.

Our backgrounds were, on the surface, enormously different. I was from a family with roots in the rural South going back many generations. My father was an orthodontist. My mother, an intensely creative woman, worked at home and in the community during the years my two brothers and I were growing up.

Alberto had been raised in Carlsbad, New Mexico, in a largely Spanish-speaking community. His father was a lay minister in the Apostolic church and worked as a janitor in Carlsbad. His mother parented Alberto and his seven sisters.

Alberto left Carlsbad in 1969 to attend high school during his junior and senior years in Northfield, Minnesota. He was a participant in "A Better Chance," a scholarship program for minority youth. While he was in Northfield, his family moved to Dinuba, California. Alberto returned to California for college. He eventually attended Fresno Pacific Mennonite Brethren College, where he began his association with the Mennonite church.

Two weeks after we married, Alberto and I moved to Minneapolis, Minnesota, where Alberto was enrolled in law school at the University. I had accepted a teaching position in the rural town of Chaska, about 30 miles from Minneapolis.

Alberto and I decided to find a Mennonite church to attend. Alberto's experience at Fresno Pacific College had been largely positive. He discovered that many people from the Mennonite church were deeply concerned with social and economic justice issues. In the small Mennonite college community, he found an outlet for his social and justice concerns, involving himself in college leadership and in organizations such as the United Farmworkers Union.

I had been raised in the southern Methodist Church (now the United Methodist Church). My faith in church communities had been shaken by the response of most white Protestant churches in the South to the civil rights movement.

I did not understand all the issues of justice and nonviolent resistance that fed that great groundswell of protest. But my parents had encouraged our interest in other peoples and other cultures. They believed that segregation had to come to an end. They had welcomed a young exchange student from Bogota, Colombia, into our home when I was 15 years old, and Maria had become like the sister I did not have. My mother's dearest friend had spent her entire adult life in Japan. When I was 17, my parents allowed me to travel to Japan to spend the summer with Cornelia.

My parents had opened windows to the world. I longed for a church community which shared a similar desire for cultural exchange and the peaceful coexistence of our global community's many different peoples. After Alberto's stories of the Mennonite church, I was willing to give it a try.

I will never forget our first Saturday night in Minneapolis. Alberto took down the yellow page directory and looked up the subheading *Mennonite*, under *Churches*. I thought this was a unique way to look for a church, but it was efficient.

We found we wouldn't have to hunt far. There were only two Mennonite churches in the Twin Cities. One was the Mennonite Brethren Church of New Hope, located about 15 minutes away from our apartment. We headed for the New Hope church on Sunday morning. There, we were met with an overwhelming friendliness that quickly convinced us to attend. We met a young couple about our age who were being married in a month. We were even invited to their wedding. Mike and Terry Scheller were to become good friends.

We were a part of the Mennonite Brethren Church of New Hope for our first four years in Minnesota. During the first year, we lived in an apartment near the University in Minneapolis. The following year, we moved out to Chaska, where I continued to teach. Alberto commuted to law school, finishing in December 1979.

That same month, we learned I was pregnant. In January 1980, Alberto was hired by the Minnesota Attorney General's office. His job would begin in March, after the February bar exam. Since his new job would be in St. Paul, we decided to look for our first house there.

I would take a maternity leave from teaching after the school year ended, and we wanted our home to be close to Alberto's work. We had both had enough of commuting 30 miles between job or school and home. We had visions of living, working, worshiping and raising our children in the same community. An upwardly mobile lifestyle, commuting between work in the city and home in the suburb, did not appeal to us.

We decided to look for our first house in a small urban community two miles south of downtown St. Paul, called the West Side. This was a neighborhood of old homes and apartments, populated by people from both Hispanic and Anglo backgrounds.

We were eager to join an urban neighborhood where we could be involved in community programs and revitalization projects. We wanted our children to experience people from both our cultural heritages. We wanted them to learn about the uniqueness and treasures of each culture. We knew that the city would be the best place for the kind of interethnic, community-centered lifestyle we envisioned.

We found our home along a quiet street, two blocks from a playground and park. We moved into the house on Baker Street in April. It had a small yard where I could imagine a garden. The house had been restored a few years previously. One room had already been decorated as a small child's room. Into this room, we moved the borrowed crib from our dear friends in Chaska, Jim and Linda Shermock.

We added the rocker that my mother had given me

when we were married. She had rocked all three of her children in it, and I was looking forward to rocking my little one between its smooth arms of cherry wood from the mountains near our home in South Carolina.

The school year ended in early June, and I tackled the house and the weed-choked garden as Alberto became involved in his job as a new attorney. He and other professional Hispanics had formed the Minnesota Hispanic Chamber of Commerce to give support and resources to Hispanic businesspeople. During the summer, he devoted much of his time and energy outside of work to planning for this organization.

During the summer, we also changed churches. Our new home in St. Paul was quite a distance from the New Hope church. We were now closer to Faith Mennonite Church, a General Conference and Mennonite Church congregation in Minneapolis.

Since Faith Church was located in an urban community, we felt we would have much in common with its participants. Changing church communities was not easy for me. I would sorely miss my friends in the New Hope church, especially Mike and Terry Scheller.

Yet Alberto had begun to devote some energy to the fledgling Hispanic Ministries department in the General Conference Mennonite Church. Our New Hope pastor had encouraged Alberto to meet Myron Schrag, the pastor at Faith church. He told Alberto of the General Conference's increasing commitment to Hispanic ministries. Alberto admired Myron, and was convinced that we should visit his urban congregation.

Joseph Alberto, our first son, was born on August 28, 1980. We felt richly blessed by his arrival! We brought him home to the house on Baker Street, which I had spent the whole summer preparing for us. We were convinced that life's greatest joy was receiving our first-born child.

We felt in those days much like any young couple in our situation. We didn't realize the effect my strikingly fair-skinned and Alberto's wonderfully dark-skinned appearance was having on others. We thought of our differences as blessings and of Joseph as a child of reconciliation. We rarely noticed people's stares and did not contemplate their reactions to us. We went about the business of our lives, intensely interested in people and their lives in our urban community. We were convinced we had found the perfect community in which to raise a child that was both Hispanic and Anglo.

The following year, my twenty-eighth and Joseph's first, I will always remember with very mixed emotions. Joseph's happy nature was a constant source of strength. I don't know how we would have faced what was to come without his joyful little face to remind us that we were blessed even in the midst of terror. Joseph had a little smile around his mouth even during his first days. I used to tell him that he must still hear the angels singing. He shared the hope of their song with us even through the dark, chaotic nights ahead.

2

"My days have passed, my plans are shattered,
and so are the desires of my heart" (Job 17:11).

A year after Joseph's birth, almost to the day, I stood in the ashes of our garage, burned by an arsonist in the night. My eyes wandered painfully over the remnants of all the precious things that we had kept in our only storage space. The small crib that we had first used for Joseph was gone, except for part of its white posts. The crib had been an heirloom that belonged to our dear friends in Chaska; it had held all their babies. They had lovingly loaned it to us as a sign of our inclusion in their family circle.

Alberto, I, and our friends Michael and Terry Scheller had so often used the big old tent. It had belonged to my family when I was growing up and had seen many an Appalachian summer when I was a young girl. It had been shelter for Alberto and me on a month's camping trip before Joseph was born, as we traveled to the Southwest in search of his birthplace and the sites of the Southwestern United States. Now it was a charred pile of blackened canvas.

All our other camping supplies were gone with the flames in the night. My new bike, which Alberto had given me, and to which I had attached a new seat for Joseph, was blackened and ruined. All our tools and garden equipment were lost. Our car was burned beyond repair. It sat alongside the ruins of the garage, where some brave fire fighter had driven it out of the burning garage the night before. The firemen had been anxious to thoroughly douse it with water before the gas tank could catch fire, endangering our home and the home next door.

Suddenly, out of my numb pain, I caught sight of a charred box. I moved over to examine it closely, as if in the middle of a slow, excruciating dream. I knew what it was. It held all my childhood Christmas ornaments. My mother had packed them and given to me when Alberto and I were married. It held the Christmas stocking she had brought home for me when I was no more than three years old. It held all the little ornaments and trinkets given to me each year by the children I taught in Chaska.

My hand reached down to open up the box, as if needing to see the remains to believe that these things, too, were gone. As my hand pushed back the charred lid, a miracle of color greeted my eyes. They were drenched with water. But the ornaments and trinkets, and yes, even the felt stocking, were perfectly preserved. I sat down beside the box and wept.

The insurance adjuster who was there with me walked over to me and put her hand on my head.

"It's alright," she said, "we can restore these things. Just give them to me and I'll take them to be cleaned. They can even take the odor of smoke out of them."

I gave her the box. In that moment, it seemed to me

as if my life was totally dependent on the care and concern of mere strangers—the fire fighters, the insurance adjusters who walked amid the ashes, the neighbors who came in and out of the yard with food or comfort or just plain curiosity.

I felt strangely detached from what had happened, as if this experience was just a bad page in our story. Someone would surely soon turn it. I kept reminding myself that the house, at least, still stood. Joseph was safe.

But even that refrain seemed empty. I couldn't be sure this page would be turned. I had heard the arson investigator say that one of our neighbor's comments on the fire was, "Well, it should have been a bomb!" I knew that if we didn't leave this house, a bomb might truly be next.

That day, standing in the ashes of our material treasures, I said good-bye to our home. I wanted to be gone from that place as soon as possible. I wanted to go far away. I wanted to tear the past year's page out of our story and go back to normal living.

I have a very wise friend who once said, "Everyone tries to tell you in times such as this that things will eventually get back to normal. But 'normal' never comes. Your life is forever changed. There is only going on from here."

How true these words seem to me. I spent many years trying to get back to a "normal" life after the arson fire. But finally I can say that this journey stretches out ever before us. There is no going back, there is no ripping the pages from our stories. There is no healthy way to stop the flood of grief and stem the loss.

As theologian Letty Russell says, we can only "keep on keepin' on." But "keepin' on" was a struggle for a very long time after the fire and through the experience of hatred and prejudice it represented.

Yet streams of grief run to meet streams of grace. It was in the midst of this stream of fear and loss that I began to long for the streams of God's gracious waters. In this struggle, I had to seek God seriously or deny that God existed at all. Graciously, the seeds of faith planted by my family and by my earliest faith community took root. They sprouted even amidst my struggle with the evil that first burned through our material treasure, then eventually threatened to consume our marriage and our child as well.

In the midst of that struggle, I began to sense the presence of a companion Struggler—one who was struggling on my behalf, and on behalf of my husband and child. I did not know why that Struggler was there or who it was that struggled for me and with me. The Struggler was made externally evident to me by the Mennonite community of faith and by the family and friends who drew close to me during my wrestling.

I was wholly engaged with the evil that threatened to destroy all that was precious to me. My eyes saw only this threat, my ears heard only its deception, and my hands and feet were locked in its grip. I struggled with all my being. I was afraid to let go or to look away. I was tempted to believe that its power was ultimate. If there had been no community of faith to surround me and minister to me, I would not have acknowledged the Struggler. But the truth of the Struggler's presence finally pierced evil's illusion that I wrestled alone.

In the beginning, the Struggler and I were side by side. Eventually, I grew tired and unable to struggle any longer. The Struggler wrestled on through the night, finally holding the darkness at bay. All I could see was the Struggler's back. Then, when the evil was held back, the Struggler turned round. I revived enough to feel rage and despair. Now I raged at the Struggler—who patiently endured.

This story is a testimony to the Struggler, who struggles for us and with us, and to the Struggler's love and great endurance. Such a one wrestled with Jacob at Peniel, on the banks of the Jabbok (Genesis 32). We do not walk away from such an encounter with God unscathed. Jacob walked away with his hip out of joint. In the story of his struggle with God, Jacob's redemption is evidenced in the flesh (his limp) and in his relationship with Esau. He is grasped by God and enfolded in the arms of his brother.

This is the image I have of the streams of grace: wrestling in the grip of a God whose love will not easily give me up—and being enfolded in the arms of my sister. With such love have I been equipped to face the struggles of my days and the suffering of a groaning creation.

3

In the spring of 1980, when I was pregnant with Joseph, it did not take us long to locate the house we wanted. In fact, the house on Baker Street, on the West Side of St. Paul, was the second one we looked at.

Alberto entered the house first, with our realtor behind him and I in the rear. As I climbed the outer stairs, I heard Alberto saying emphatically, "This is it!"

I couldn't believe it. The house looked awkward from the outside. I had almost said, "No!" from the curbside. It was a tall two-story home that sat on one side of a narrow city lot, not two yards from the neighboring house on the east side. There were no shrubs or trees to soften its appearance, and all the old Dutch elms on the street had died from disease. The house was weather-beaten and did not appeal to me at all.

As I entered, however, I began to understand Alberto's excitement—although I had never seen him react so emotionally to something he hardly knew anything about. It was obvious someone had carefully restored the inside of the house, which now looked somewhat dirty and neglected. Our realtor informed us that the house had been vacant for several months.

I warmed to the house when I saw the newly carpeted living and dining areas and the beautifully restored kitchen. The kitchen was large and filled with the afternoon sun. I could envision our expected child playing happily on the floor while I worked.

There was a small study downstairs and four rooms upstairs. The child's room was small and filled with sunlight, like the kitchen below. I had to agree with Alberto. This house had the potential to become our first.

We signed the purchase agreement and applied for a loan. Then we went through a month of excitement over our prospective home and agony over rising interest rates. We finally heard that we had qualified for an FHA loan. At the same time, interest rates dropped. We couldn't believe our good fortune. We closed on the house and packed up our belongings in Chaska.

We spent the two weekends before we moved cleaning and making minor repairs on our new house. Jim Shermock, our friend from Chaska, dug up six saplings from his woods and brought them over. He and Alberto planted the young trees in our yard. I could imagine them growing taller with our growing child, providing branches for climbing and for shade.

We met some of our neighbors. A single man, Stan, owned the house that bordered ours on the east side. We met John Robinson, who owned the house on the west side of ours, when Alberto went over to borrow a plumber's wrench. John offered to come and help Alberto turn our water on. We learned he was married, with six children ranging in age from about 11 to 20.

We also met Mrs. Brown, an elderly woman across the street. Mrs. Brown was friendly and told us a little about the neighborhood and its history. She and her husband had raised their family in her home, which rested on a double lot.

We moved in on a weekend in mid-April 1980. The next six weeks were busy. I commuted back to Chaska each day to finish up the school year, while Alberto worked in the Attorney General's office and with the Hispanic Chamber of Commerce. We both missed friends in Chaska. But we were looking forward to becoming involved in our new urban community.

After school was out in June, my parents drove up from South Carolina, pulling a trailer full of furniture. They brought the dining room set with which my maternal grandparents had set up housekeeping. Nanny, as we called my mother's mother, had stored the set for us when she moved from her home to an apartment.

My parents also brought my childhood bedroom furniture. It was wonderful to put into place these pieces which held so many memories for me. They helped make our house on Baker Street truly home.

My parents stayed a week, helping us unpack all the things we had left boxed since April. Mama Wells had also brought a box filled with wedding gifts we had not been able to bring on our first move to Minnesota. Unboxing those gifts brought back the face of each person who had given them.

The week with my parents was filled with work and joy, especially over their expected grandchild. When Mama and Daddy Wells got in their car to leave, tears filled my eyes. I was used to saying good-bye to them. But suddenly I realized that, next time I saw them, I would be a mother. Mom hugged me tightly and stepped bravely into the car.

The summer went by swiftly. My expanding size

and weeks of intense heat, unusual for Minnesota, prevented my working in the garden. I worked at meeting people in our neighborhood and in our new church.

I met Cathy O'Brien, who lived on our block. She was a friendly young woman with three children, one of whom was an infant. Her husband, Michael, was a truck driver. They had moved to the neighborhood about a year earlier. I also met a woman who was to become a special friend. Shelley lived many blocks from us and had a little boy who was a year old. She came over for lunch one day, and I could tell right away that she was a person I might befriend.

While we were beginning to feel at home in our new community, several disconcerting incidents happened. One day in late spring, we came home to find two sections of the fence between our home and the Robinson's shattered. The fence was weathered, made in seven sections. Each section contained three upright posts with horizontal slats between them.

Eighteen-year-old Greg Robinson told Alberto the fence had blown down. If the fence was that rickety, maybe we should consider putting up a new one. We had realized when we bought the house that the fence would need to be replaced within a year or two. We had hoped we would not need a new one so soon.

Alberto went over to talk to John Robinson about putting up a new fence together. John was in the construction business. He had power tools in his garage and lumber stacked in the yard. If we pooled resources, a new fence would not be too big an expense.

John was not at home, but his wife, Brenda, was. Alberto talked to Brenda and came back perplexed. He sat down and shared the conversation. When he had mentioned that he wanted to discuss building a new fence together, Brenda had begun yelling at him, saying, "We're not going to build a new fence. We bought that fence and told Sam [the previous owner of our home] to put up a good fence!"

I too was perplexed. Alberto and I decided that if the fence was an emotional issue, we wouldn't pursue it. Alberto would repair the broken fence as best he could. Later we could buy a new one ourselves. So Alberto took a large jar of nails and a hammer and, over two weeks, repaired the fence. Several times, while Alberto worked on the fence, Brenda Robinson sat out in her backyard drinking beer.

She became verbally abusive. "Why are you building that stupid fence?" she screamed at Alberto, adding a string of obscenities. "I told Sam to buy a good fence! You should buy a good fence and put it up."

Alberto worked on quietly, assuming Brenda was intoxicated.

During the summer, the Robinsons had several loud beer parties in their backyard that lasted into early morning. Several times Alberto walked over to request that the party be a little quieter. The Robinsons and their friends would offer Alberto a beer and agree to quiet down, but the volume never decreased.

We accepted this behavior because we didn't want to offend the Robinsons. We often heard them yelling and cursing at each other in their home or in their yard. They used offensive language even when not angry. Cursing was a habit. Some days that summer, I would hear them start to argue in midmorning, and the argument would resurface throughout the day. The heat required us to keep our windows opened; I could hear each word only too plainly.

It is hard for those who live on large suburban lots with central air-conditioning to realize how close to each other people live in older urban communities. Urban lots are tiny, and houses can almost adjoin one another. Furthermore, in summer heat most folks must open all windows to catch what breeze there is.

As a result, one household almost lives with the neighboring ones. This can be pleasant for those of us who love urban areas and are excited about building up neighborhoods and communities of caring.

However, the individualistic nature of our culture makes it difficult for us to understand how greatly the actions of our own households affect the households of others. Many times during the summer of 1980, Alberto and I would sit down to supper after he had spent a hard day at work, and an argument would start up in the Robinson's backyard. It seemed as if they were right there at our table. We longed for escape from the yelling and obscene language going on unchecked next door. On a few occasions, we changed into swimsuits and drove to a nearby lake to swim and enjoy the peace of a park.

Our busy lives and the approaching birth of our child kept us from paying too much attention to the Robinson's lifestyle. As August drew near, we got the baby's room ready. We started childbirth classes.

Finally the time came. I labored eight hours and had been in the delivery room another two hours when it became apparent I would need Cesarean delivery. Alberto was allowed into the surgical room. I was given spinal anesthesia so I would be awake and alert for the birth. Joseph was born at a healthy seven pounds, and he was placed in Alberto's arms right away.

I looked at this screaming child, and felt how miraculous life really is. I was grateful for the surgical procedure that preserved both my life and Joseph's. I appreciated my physician's great concern that we be allowed to participate in this birth as fully as possible. Joseph was placed by my side and we were wheeled to the recovery room. I spent time touching and nursing him before he was taken to the nursery.

Back in my hospital room, Alberto and I called our families. My maternal grandmother, Bess Drennan, flew to Minnesota five days later. Joseph and I were still in the hospital, so Alberto brought Nanny from the airport to our hospital room. She put on a gown and came in to hold her great-grandson. We have pictures of her holding Joseph proudly. In one picture, he has one of his enchanting smiles on his tiny face.

My mother arrived the day after Joseph and I came home. She and my grandmother took good care of all three of us. My father arrived a week later, and we spent a joyous weekend together. When they all flew home, we knew we would miss them. But Alberto and I were also eager to begin our lives as a family of three. It seemed as if dreams of a lifetime were being fulfilled.

4

Our first two months as new parents were the excited, anxious ones most young parents experience. Joseph grew from what seemed a fragile newborn into a sturdy, small baby. Friends came to visit us and to see Joseph. We took him and spent a day with our friends, the Shermocks, in Chaska.

At the end of September, our church gave us a baby shower. The shower was on a Saturday night, and included all members of the church families. It was an evening that reinforced our feelings of being supported in our new role as parents by the Faith Mennonite Church community.

The days went swiftly that fall. Alberto was in his permanent assignment with the Attorney General's office, in the commerce division. The Minnesota Hispanic Chamber of Commerce would officially open for membership in November. I was busy caring for Joseph and gaining back strength lost from the surgical delivery.

I looked forward to Alberto's return in the evenings, and Alberto seemed just as eager to get home to us. He played with and cared for Joseph each evening. I watched a very close relationship develop between Alberto and our little son. We were learning to be a family of three.

However, the Robinsons were once again intruding on our lives. Early in the fall, John and his sons began to construct a screened-in patio house, midway between their house and their unattached garage. The foundation for the screen house was poured on the property line between our lot and theirs. Much later, we learned that John was violating building codes by putting the foundation right on our property line and adding an additional building on his small lot. At the time, we were not familiar with this regulation.

John and his sons proceeded to put up the frame and prepare the new building to be stuccoed. Of course, the construction was not a quiet affair. Each evening, and late into many nights, they would hammer away, talking, arguing, shouting, cursing.

We were privately upset that the Robinsons had not told us they were going to build their screen house. It came at a difficult time for us. Joseph was still sleeping in the room off our bedroom, which faced the back of our house and the construction. The hammering and shouting occasionally woke him up. I was forced to close the windows when it was cool enough, or to run the fan to block some of the noise when it was warm.

The hammering and shouting often accompanied our supper hour and interfered with our sleep. As the fall wore on, I felt more and more worn down. I was getting up to nurse Joseph twice in the night, and because of the pounding and hammering, was unable to sleep in the afternoons or to go to bed early at night. Alberto was also beginning to feel the strain of work and too little sleep. He talked to the Robinsons about keeping the noise down and restricting the construction to reasonable hours and times. Abusive language met his requests.

Finally work ceased on the screen house. But the Robinsons tacked tar paper to the back of the screen house and did not stucco it. The uncompleted screen house was an eye-sore from our side of the fence. Alberto talked with John and his sons, asking them to finish the screen house so that we would not be stuck with the tar papering all winter. Again they responded with abusive language.

After completing the side facing their property, the Robinsons moved a telephone and television set into the screen house. Early in the day, Brenda used both constantly, and the kids did so after school or work. We could clearly hear their telephone ring in our home. Several times when we had friends over, the Robinson's phone rang and our friends asked why we didn't answer our phone. We would wearily explain. Their television blared most of the day, tuned to game shows and soap operas. At night, the screen house hosted youth parties which often involved alcohol.

Our nerves were wearing thin. We began to go through bottles of aspirin because Alberto suffered from constant headaches and backaches. Looking at photos taken in November 1980, I am taken aback at how thin and haggard I look.

Nevertheless, we were determined that the Robinsons would not control our lives. We enjoyed Joseph each day, realizing that children grow all too quickly. We spent time with friends. I planned a week's visit home to South Carolina in early November. My brothers had not yet seen Joseph. My paternal grandmother was ailing physically, and I wanted her to see Joseph and to have the opportunity to hold him.

We spent Thanksgiving with the Shermocks, our friends in Chaska. Jim and Linda had three children. They have always made room for us at family holiday gatherings. Joseph, as usual, enjoyed the festivities. He was a very sociable baby, his dark brown eyes sparkling as he oohed and aahed at our attentions. He was already beginning to give to us a measure of the love that we were giving him.

5

Winter brought a reprieve from the Robinson's harrassment. Because of Minnesota temperatures, they were forced to move their activities out of the uninsulated screen house. From November through March, we no longer heard their arguments, television, or phone conversations. We began to relax and to forget what life with the Robinsons was like.

In January, we visited Alberto's family in California. It was the first time that Alberto's parents, his seven sisters, and their families had seen Joseph. We had a wonderful trip. We visited Fresno Pacific College, Alberto's alma mater. As we drove along the San Joaquin valley, Joseph sleeping soundly in his car seat, we talked and dreamed about coming to the valley to live one day. The warm climate and the small farms tucked away in the foothills attracted us.

We spun dreams in the secure context of the small car as we drove through the valley. Imaginary tapestries were woven and unraveled in the relaxed atmosphere of those days of travel. I thought, at the time, that the reason we had not talked like this for months was because of Alberto's work, my recovery from childbirth, our care for the baby. Looking back, I know that our home in Minnesota was becoming a place too tense in which to share carefree dreams.

We returned to St. Paul and our busy lives. I was glad to be home and back into the routine Joseph and I shared. The winter was unusually warm for Minnesota. Some days I would bundle Joseph into our chest carrier and take him for a walk.

One day, Joseph and I saw Mrs. Davis, an elderly woman who lived two doors down from us, out shoveling her walk. I stopped to chat. Mrs. Davis said she was not feeling well. She had been hospitalized earlier the previous fall and said that she still did not feel "like my old self." She was not yet able to drive her car.

Later, back in the house, I began to be concerned about Mrs. Davis. She seemed depressed from being indoors so much. Her son brought her groceries regularly. But in the long Minnesota winter, it's important to get out once in a while to avoid cabin fever.

The next day I was baking bread. On impulse, I took a loaf to Mrs. Davis, staying to talk briefly. I asked her if she would enjoy going grocery shopping with me and Joseph once a week. She seemed to welcome the opportunity, and we settled on a time for our first trip.

Mrs. Davis became a good friend. She often treated me to a sandwich before or after our shopping. Many times, she pushed Joseph in the grocery cart while I shopped. He became very comfortable with her, giggling and smiling as she talked to him.

The winter brought other significant community involvements for us. In late January, I joined a small baby-sitting co-op in our West Side community, along with Shelley, my close friend. The baby-sitting co-op had been started by eight women who had also helped open the West Side Food Co-op.

The baby-sitting co-op was to become an important network of support for me as a parent at home. The co-op operated on an exchange of hours. No money was exchanged. The co-op provided quality childcare for Joseph and socialization with other children while I did volunteer work or met with a friend for lunch. The women in our co-op got together one evening a month, so we came to know one another well.

We made another commitment on the last Sunday in February, when Alberto and I became members of Faith Mennonite Church. That Sunday we also dedicated Joseph, committing ourselves to nurture him in Christian faith, supported by the whole congregation.

Joining the church was an important covenant for us. We had discussed taking the step for several years. Thus on this cold Sunday morning, Alberto and I drove toward church with butterflies. We were both prepared to make statements of commitment to our congregation and were rehearsing these on the way.

Suddenly Alberto said, "Now . . . what were you—Baptist?"

"Methodist!" I replied. "We were married in the Methodist church, remember?"

"Methodist! That's right," Alberto exclaimed. "Well, it doesn't matter. After today, you'll be a Mennonite."

So, on February 22, 1981, Alberto and I together entered the Mennonite church. Joseph's dedication was a moving experience for us. I had been baptized as an infant. But I had come to agree with the Mennonite belief that baptism should be an outward sign of a person's decision to follow Christ as a disciple. This decision could only be made when a person was old enough to understand and accept Christ's salvation for our lives.

I appreciated the beautiful service of dedication that presented Joseph to our church family and asked for their support and love for him. After the brief dedication, the congregation sang, "He's Got the Whole World in His Hands." One verse, sung especially for our son, was "He's got Joseph Alberto in his hands." I continued to sing that song with its special verse for Joseph just before he went to sleep each night.

By winter's end, Alberto and I were feeling part of our neighborhood and our church communities. We valued the challenges and opportunities that urban life provided. Joseph was growing rapidly. We quietly celebrated his first six months. He was creeping by the end of February, mostly in reverse. I took him swimming regularly at a downtown, indoor pool. I had become an avid swimmer during my pregnancy. I wanted him also to enjoy the water. Joseph continued to be happy, and Alberto and I were relaxing into parenthood.

6

The month of April brought hints of spring to Minnesota. We turned toward gardening, bicycling, and enjoying the precious, warmer weather. However, April also brought the Robinsons outside again and into the still unfinished screen house. Again we lived with the daily noise of game-shows, soap operas, telephone conversations, and drinking parties.

On the Saturday evening before Easter Sunday, we accepted an invitation from a Jewish friend of mine to share Passover supper with her and her husband. We spent a wonderful evening of fellowship, sharing in the spiritual history of the Exodus and eating the Passover meal. Joseph was the youngest male present, and Joel, our friend, solemnly said Joseph's lines in the service for him. We left about 10:00 that evening, filled with the joy of the Passover remembrance, and looking forward to Easter morning with our congregation.

When we arrived home, we noticed that Stan, our single neighbor next door on the east side, was having a quiet party. Alberto and I commented on how appropriate the noise level at this party seemed. We put Joseph to bed and went to sleep.

Suddenly, about 1:00 a.m., I wakened to the sounds of loud, angry shouting. I got up and looked out our bedroom window to see two youths, one of them 19-year-old Greg Robinson, jumping the fence between our house and Stan's. Both young men landed right in the garden I had just planted. They ran through the garden, across our yard, and then, unbelievably, smashed their way through the wooden fence Alberto had spent so much time repairing.

At my cries, Alberto came to the window to see Greg and his friend trample several sections of the fence and step into the Robinson's yard. All the while, Greg and his buddy were yelling over their shoulders, cursing at the people who had now gathered in Stan's backyard. We stood stunned at our window.

We returned to bed, remembering that this was now Easter morning. Alberto commented tiredly that we would see about the fence later. We were both awakened a short time later by the sound of tires screeching in our back alley and more loud, angry voices. Jumping up to look out our window, we saw several police cars in the back alley and police officers in Stan's yard.

As I watched, one police officer pulled his gun out, dropped to his knees, and yelled for everyone in the yard to freeze. Greg was back in Stan's yard and was refusing to obey the police order. He stood there, cursing loudly at the officer, until another officer pushed him to the ground. The police put Greg into a squad car, and the party at Stan's home began to break up.

Meanwhile, one of the officers walked over to our yard to survey the damaged fence. Alberto put on a robe and went down to talk to the officer. The officer asked if Alberto wanted to press charges for destruction of property. Alberto said yes.

Suddenly, John Robinson came running out of his back door, yelling at the police officer and at Alberto, "That's my fence, and my boys damaged it and I don't want to press charges!"

The police officer asked Alberto who owned the fence. Alberto answered that ownership was obviously unclear, so he would not press charges.

Alberto came back to bed, exhausted and worried. The earlier peacefulness of the Passover meal was gone and Easter morning was marred. We went to bed, hoping that eventually our racing hearts would stop pounding.

We woke up tired and disconcerted. We were responsible for serving part of an early breakfast at church, so there wasn't much time to talk about what had happened. Still, it was difficult to shake off the feelings of shock and dread even on this joyous occasion. We shared the incident with some friends at church, but we didn't want to dwell on the details.

We arrived home in early afternoon. Soon afterward, there was a knock on the door. Stan had come to apologize for the disturbance.

"We saw your party when we got home last night. We noticed how quiet it was," Alberto and I assured Stan. We told him we had been awakened by the shouting that accompanied Greg Robinsons's dash through our backyard and fence.

Stan shared his concerns over what had happened Saturday night. He told us that Greg and 16-year-old Tom Robinson, along with two friends, had entered his home through the front door about 10:00 p.m. They had crashed into his living room, already intoxicated, and demanded some beer.

"I tried to get them to leave," Stan said.

Greg became very belligerent, saying to Stan, "Look, you don't give a party in our neighborhood without inviting me."

Finally Stan persuaded them to go home. But later they returned and began to antagonize Stan's guests. Some pushing and shoving ensued, after which Greg and one buddy left the party through our backyard. Greg returned to the party through the alley with a knife. He pulled the knife on one of Stan's friends. Stan called the police, who arrested Greg for assault. Stan's friend had signed the arrest charges.

Stan was concerned about retaliation from Greg. "I'm afraid of Greg. He's very unpredictable when he's drunk."

We shared with Stan some of the daily incidents we had experienced with the Robinson family. The three of us agreed that it might be wise to call a neighborhood meeting to discuss these concerns with the Robinsons, if they would agree to come. We also agreed to call on each other in the future when we needed support.

On the Monday morning following Easter, Alberto and I woke Joseph up at 5:30 a.m. We drove to the hospital for a surgical circumcision the baby's pediatrician and a urologist had determined needed to be done. The procedure was to be completed on an outpatient basis, but we both felt anxious about the administration of anesthetic and the surgery for one so young.

The circumcision and recovery period were to take about an hour, but because of complications, we were at the hospital most of the day. We arrived home completely exhausted by the emotions and anxiety of the past hours. We ate supper and all three fell fast asleep in our large bed upstairs. Alberto and I needed the comfort of Joseph's small body safely between ours.

Tuesday, April 21, Joseph bore witness to the incredible healing capacity of infants. He was sore but lively! I was relieved to have the experience behind us. That night, I nursed Joseph. After he fell asleep, I settled down to sleep beside him.

A party was gearing up in the Robinson's screen house, and I was unable to fall asleep. All the tension and exhaustion of the past few days overwhelmed me. I jumped up, telling Alberto I was going to call the Robinson's house and ask for some quiet.

I dialed their number and a young person answered. I asked to speak to Brenda or to John.

The youth asked belligerently, "Who is this?" Again I requested to speak to Brenda or to John.

"Who is this?" the voice demanded once more.

I gave up. "Who am I talking to?" I asked.

"This is Greg!"

"Well, Greg, this is your neighbor, Helen Quintela. Greg, we have been disturbed twice this week by you and your friends. Our baby is recovering from some surgery, and we all need sleep. I wonder if you and your friends. . ."

I didn't get any farther. Greg began to yell and curse into the phone, screaming, "Your worthless coward of a husband put me in jail Saturday night!"

By this time, Alberto was standing near the phone, and I handed it to him. Greg was still yelling and cursing. Alberto asked him to calm down.

"If you want to ask me to quiet down, you come over here and do it face-to-face. Don't be calling me on the phone!" Greg shrieked, drowning Alberto in obscenities.

Alberto calmly told Greg that he was going to call the police. "I'll ask for a police officer to accompany me to your house so we can talk."

Alberto hung up and dialed the police. He explained the situation to the sergeant on duty and requested that a police officer come to our home and help mediate. Suddenly, before Alberto could hang up, there was a pounding on our front screen door.

Greg was yelling and cursing, daring Alberto to come out and "fight like a man." Alberto and I looked at each other, horrified. It sounded as if the aluminum storm door would not hold up. Once inside the storm door, he would be on our small front porch and next to the oak front door with its glass window. I think we both had visions of Greg smashing through the window and being loose in our home.

The police sergeant was still on the line. I heard Alberto say nervously, "Greg is out on my front steps screaming and pounding on my door. It sounds like he might break the door down. I'm going to go and ask him to get off my property and to go home, but I think I'll need some assistance."

Alberto handed me the phone and walked over to our front door with the large window. He looked at Greg, who was still pounding on the storm door. Alberto opened the oak door, entering our front porch. Greg continued to pound, yelling and cursing.

I remember begging the police sergeant to stay on the line until the squad car arrived. I was terrified, and the sergeant's reassuring voice did little to comfort me. I wondered if Greg had his knife with him and what he would do if he could get past that storm door to Alberto. The hatred and insanity in Greg's voice was horrifying.

I could hear Alberto telling Greg over and over to go home, that we had called the police, and that he should return to his house before the police arrived. Greg's brother Tom and a friend were now behind Greg on the sidewalk, watching wordlessly. Alberto was telling them to take Greg home.

After what seemed an eternity, Greg quieted down, and his brother and friend were able to talk to him. They asked Greg to go home. Alberto unlocked and opened the storm door slightly. Since the door opened outwardly, Greg had to back down the steps, toward his brother and friend.

Suddenly, the squad car arrived. Greg glanced at it. Then he turned back toward Alberto, and lunged at him with a fierce scream. A police officer jumped from the squad car, grabbed Greg, and pulled him down the steps. He ordered Greg to leave our yard. Greg began to yell and curse at the officer, who then handcuffed him and put him into the squad car.

The police officer came into our house to bring us the arrest papers. He explained that he could not take Greg into police headquarters unless we signed arrest charges for trespassing and disorderly conduct. Alberto and I realized that Greg was probably intoxicated. From our experience Saturday and then again this night, we believed Greg was dangerous when drunk. We realized Greg would be home the next day on bail, but we also knew that by morning he would be sober and no longer violent. We signed the papers.

By this time, Joseph was awake. I quieted him and the police officer left with Greg. Alberto and I, with Joseph, wearily climbed the stairs to go to bed for the second time that night.

Incredibly, as we reached our bedroom, we heard a loud pounding on our back door. The fear of a short time ago rose up in me. For an irrational moment, I thought Greg must be back. Then we heard John Robinson, Greg's father, screaming up at us from the side yard, directing his voice to the side window of the small room adjoining our bedroom.

John yelled out, "You little nigger, I'll get you. I'll beat you up everytime you walk out your front door, nigger."

We walked over to the window. When John saw Alberto, his voice rose. I gently pushed Alberto back out of John's sight and opened the window. I asked John if he would give me a chance to tell him what had happened.

I said to him, "John, I'm scared. You're frightening me. Will you just let me talk to you a minute.?"

John immediately looked contrite. "You don't have to be frightened," he said.

I then proceeded to relate the night's incidents to John. As I talked to him, a police officer appeared beside John, out of the dark. He and his partner had been passing by and had heard John yelling.

The officer looked up at me. "Is everything alright?" he asked.

I requested that he and John come to our front porch, where we could all talk together. John agreed, and the police officers accompanied him to the porch. I finished relating the night's events to John.

After I finished, John said, "Well, if Greg's done wrong, he should pay the consequences."

Alberto started to say something, but John cut him off. "You're all mad about that fence. It was just a little mistake. I'll fix the dumb fence!"

It became obvious that John would relate to me, but harbored much anger toward Alberto. Both Greg and John seemed irrationally to hold Alberto responsible for Greg's arrest Saturday night.

One of the officers told John, "You are responsible for controlling Greg." He added, "It's time for you to leave and let these people get some sleep."

John agreed and we all parted. I was hopeful that John might make an effort to control Greg. I was aware that John had intensely negative, racially biased feelings toward Alberto. Still, I hoped John would realize how wrong Greg's actions were.

I had never experienced a family system characterized by abuse and chemical dependency. I still believed logic and rational behavior would prevail in the Robinson's household and in our relationship to them. I believed people basically abhor violence. I had never personally experienced hatred fed by racial discrimination and violence.

But we were now locked into a cycle that was to become more and more destructive in its patterns. A family that had for years victimized one another now turned their self-hatred onto us. We were an interethnic family that could easily be a target for the gang of friends who almost nightly hung out drinking at the Robinson's screen house.

We were becoming powerless in the face of an enmity that hated because of who we were. Some members of the Robinson family were no less victims than we. But, trapped for years in such a cycle, all members of the family united in their irrational opposition to us. We began, after this night, to descend into hell.

7

In April, after the incident with Gary and John's tirade, we began to speak to neighbors. We asked them to help us deal with the growing problem of our relationship to the Robinsons. We suggested that we have a neighborhood meeting. The Robinsons would be invited, and we could all discuss our needs for safety and peace on our inner-city block.

We hoped to set common guidelines for late-night parties in our neighborhood. There had been other incidents that concerned people. A prowler had been spotted in a back alley late one night, and the windshield of a car parked on the street had been smashed.

We were not prepared for the varied responses of our neighbors. Some harbored great anger of their own toward the Robinson family. They felt powerless to affect any change after many years of fear. These neighbors felt for us but were too afraid to help or be associated with us.

Some neighbors staunchly defended the Robinsons. They reminded us that the Robinsons had lived on the block for 17 years—and we only one. A few hinted that we must have done something to cause the family's wrath. No one told us that Gary and his brothers had once belonged to youth gangs which harassed elderly persons. We were to learn this much later.

The hints from some that we must be somehow at fault made us wonder. Had we indeed done something to make the Robinsons hate and condemn us? We went over and over everything we had ever said to them. We remembered their helpfulness when we first moved to Baker Street. Had we made a mistake in the way we first approached them about the repair of the fence? We began to experience the silent guilt of victims who suffer the questions of the seemingly reasonable people around them. All kinds of folks suggested ways we might "show them you are good neighbors."

But as time passed and we tried harder to be good neighbors, the Robinsons' behavior became more and more irrational and destructive. We were caught in a downward spiral of shrinking self-esteem. The harder we tried to be the "right kind" of neighbors, the more dismally we failed.

In a neighborhood where "no one had ever had any problems," we had brought trouble down on everyone. In a city where there was "no significant racial tension," we had started some. In a society where "anyone is free to live anywhere," we could not seem to live on Baker Street.

So we began to ask the self-destructive question, "What, then, is wrong with us?"

In her book, *Suffering*, Dorothee Soelle describes the consciousness of being powerless as one of the fundamental elements in suffering. "Every attempt to humanize suffering must begin with this phenomenon of experienced powerlessness and must activate forces that enable a person to overcome the feeling that he [she] is without power."

47

After the incident on April 21, it became clear that the Robinson's hatred and harassment were racially motivated. Alberto was being attacked and cursed because he was a person of color. There was nothing he could do that would change the way the Robinsons perceived him. He would have had to change the color of his skin. We were powerless to stem the tide of hatred and abuse rising against us.

Such an experience of powerlessness to change the abuser's behavior, and the cycle of abuse, leads to feelings of worthlessness in the victim. The victim assumes the guilt of the abuse! Instead of seeing the responsibility as lying with the abuser, the abused believes he or she is responsible. The victim may become silent or even apathetic in the face of the abuse, an experience that is like death.

While some people refused to support us, we received encouragement of a different sort from those truly enraged over what was happening. Word began to leak out into the Hispanic community that we were being harassed and threatened. Racial and ethnic tensions that had lain dormant revived.

We began to get messages through individuals who would walk up to us at a local Mexican restaurant or on the street that "the brothers are ready. Just say the word and we'll blow them [the Robinsons] away."

We realized with mounting apprehension that there was a whole network of people ready and willing to take care of "the problem" violently. We feared that someone we didn't even know would start the street war without asking for our assent. The more we tried to explain our belief in nonviolent response, the angrier some folks became. Some, including one of our closest Hispanic friends, would become so disillusioned with us that he would abandon us completely.

Later in the summer, after a break-in and vandalism of our home, we would turn to the Crime Victim program for help. It was a new program in St. Paul, and the man who came to see us was probably as baffled and confused as we were. But he didn't admit his own feelings of powerlessness after uselessly trying to talk to the Robinsons about a mediation session.

Instead he said to me, "Well, I suggest you set up a submachine gun."

He was joking, of course. But his suggestion frightened me to the core. To suggest such power to one who is trapped, powerless, in a cycle of abuse, is to incite severe temptation to seize power from an outside source. Why not get a gun? Perhaps one night, before the police could arrive, we would need it to assure our survival.

People have such varied responses to the affliction of another. Some become angry at the afflicted one, and flee. Perhaps their anger arises from their feelings of powerlessness. Some, like our friend, become angry at the victim's unwillingness to exercise power. Or their anger may be the result of identifying with the oppressor.

I was to learn, as the months went by, that one of our neighbors was an alcoholic. On the last day in our home on Baker Street, I was sitting on the steps alongside my mother as the movers packed our belongings. This woman came and sat on the steps with us. I was filled with pain and grief, my despair spilling over in a flood of tears.

And the woman turned to me, saying, "Now get hold of yourself. You are a grown woman and here you are, crying like a baby!"

The anger of others toward the afflicted has, I believe, to do with their own fear of becoming victims. When we hear of the horrible things that happen each day in our world, we usually respond by finding a reason why the afflicted one became the victim of a certain crime or abuse.

We say to ourselves, "Well, if she hadn't been walking around like that late at night." Or we think, *I'd never leave my child unsupervised. I'd never dream of letting my child walk alone to the library*.

Yet there are, in truth, many such moments when we walk at an unwise hour down the street, or when we turn watchful eyes away from our vibrant children, who long to act independently. There are no guarantees in this world. None of us has a magic shield to protect us from the evil we have loosed on our earth.

The people who faulted us usually did so by assuming we were people who just couldn't get along with our neighbors. The most painful response to us in all the months on Baker was in the enraged voice of a Hispanic woman on the phone. The arson fire had burned our garage, automobile, and belongings. I had called to ask if her son, who owned an auto shop, could come and appraise our car for the insurance company.

She yelled, "You should know my son is too busy to come right away, especially for people who can't even get along with their neighbors."

Certainly, I thought wearily as I hung up the phone

before she could wound more deeply, *a fire that has consumed so much is an enormous price for not getting along with the neighbors.* But so deep were my wounds and so powerless did I feel, that I began to wonder, deep in my heart, if she might be right.

What was the response of our church community and our families? We were most reluctant to share our experiences and pain with the very ones who loved us the most. Why? I suppose we did not want to wound them, knowing that they would feel deeply any hurts we felt.

In addition, as our self-esteem eroded, we became more and more emotionally isolated. When we were at church, or in touch with our families, the world back at our home seemed unreal. We weren't sure it was as bad as we experienced it to be. We reasoned that if we just spent this time away and rested, everything would seem better when we returned. We began to live two lives that had little connection to one another. One was a life of irrationality and fear on Baker Street. One was a familiar life within the comforting space of our dear friends and family members.

This ability to compartmentalize feelings and events in one's life is surely a major characteristic of people who suffer. The human capacity to endure suffering is amazing. The mind "forgets" the suffering and abuse in the safe context, even if it is only in the space of day-dreams. But this ability to compartmentalize, to consciously forget, has a price. The body does not forget. Thus the afflicted inevitably become ill, even to the point of death.

But the time was to come when we could no longer

hide our suffering from our family and friends. They were to read it in our strained faces and in the loss of weight we both sustained. When we could no longer hide what was happening, they responded not with anger, nor with accusations or suggestions.

They responded in a way that was to be our salvation. They drew close to us even when we would have turned our afflicted faces away from them in shame. They began to take upon themselves the suffering that had come upon us, "taking up our infirmities and carrying our sorrows," just as the one from Nazareth did for us all two millennia ago.

8

Those who surrounded us in our trouble were drawing on the biblical understanding of God as present in the midst of our suffering. The Bible asserts that faithful people of God are to draw near to the afflicted, for whom God has great concern and compassion.

The story of the Creation and the Fall speaks of a God who has entered the broken created order. God did not abandon or destroy the creation into which evil was unleashed through disobedience. Instead, God sought the redemption of the creation and is seeking it still. Paul says this in Romans 8:

> We know that the whole creation has been groaning as in the pains of childbirth right up to the present time. Not only so, but we ourselves, who have the firstfruits of the Spirit, groan inwardly as we wait eagerly for our adoption as [children], the redemption of our bodies. . . . In the same way, the Spirit helps us in our weakness. We do not know what we ought to pray for, but the Spirit intercedes for us with groans that words cannot express.

Paul affirms the presence of God's Spirit with groaning creation and with the faithful, who groan in solidarity with the created order. Indeed, the Spirit groans for us, on our behalf, seeking and awaiting with us that final redemption. As Dorothee Soelle writes in *Suffering*,

> Redemption does not come to people from outside or from above. God wants to use people in order to work on the completion of [the] creation. Precisely for this reason God must also suffer with the creation.

This suffering of God with all creation is heard in the groaning of the Spirit that cannot be expressed in words. It is an act of solidarity. It does not give advice to the sufferer. It does not hand the victim power from the outside, thus reinforcing powerlessness. It does not offer comfort when there is no comfort. It does not even look to a future that cannot be seen.

It acknowledges the suffering. It does not turn away. It takes on suffering along with the sufferer. In its own way, this groaning from the depths of experience is the beginning of hope. The afflicted is not alone! Joy flickers in the depths of darkness.

The Old Testament witnesses to the presence of God's spirit with those who suffer and have been abandoned. The story of Joseph's sojourn in Egypt tells of God's presence with one thrown into the pit of death and sold as a slave. Genesis 39:2 declares that "The Lord was with Joseph." The Lord is alongside the betrayed and abandoned one, seeking Joseph's salvation and redemption.

The account of the sojourn in Egypt and the enslavement of the Israelites bears witness to the response of faithful people to Yahweh's constant presence. The Hebrew midwives, under penalty of death, disobeyed

Pharaoh's command to kill the male infants delivered to Hebrew women. "The midwives, however, feared God and did not do what the king of Egypt had told them to do; they let the boys live" (Exodus 1:17). The midwives stood with the mothers of Israel. They risked their lives for those born to oppression.

The story of Ruth and Naomi is testimony to a Moabite woman, a foreigner, who drew close to her mother-in-law, a sister afflicted by grief and unimaginable sorrow. Ruth carries Naomi's sorrows as they trudge together on the road back to Bethlehem.

Once they arrive, she cares for Naomi's physical needs until Naomi can respond to the needs of her daughter-in-law. At the birth of Obed, the women sing praises to the God who has renewed Naomi's life. This salvation has been effected through the ministry of Ruth, "who loves you and who is better to you than seven sons. . ." (Ruth 4:15).

The psalms of lamentation give voice to the ones who suffer and approach God with their suffering. The faithful sufferer is given a model for complaining, questioning, demanding relief. God is not a distant ruler who disdains the pleas of those on earth.

God lends an ear to the peoples of the earth. God hovers over the grieved, with wings of comfort, lifting them up and renewing their strength. God stretches out the almighty arm and compassionately extends a hand toward the ones who are afflicted. The outstretched hand of God is revealed through the ministry of the faithful to those cast down.

God's outstretched hand is a common picture of Yahweh's compassion for the afflicted. Psalm 136 gives praise and thanksgiving to the Lord, who "brought Israel out from among (Egypt) with a mighty hand and outstretched arm."

Isaiah speaks of the day that Yahweh will stretch forth his hand and "will wipe away the tears from all faces" (Isa. 25:8).

Isaiah 65 speaks of the hand of God outstretched even to those who turn away from the Almighty's comfort. "To a nation that did not call on my name, I said, 'Here am I, here am I.' All day long I have held out my hands. . . ."

The imagery of the arm and hand of the Lord speaks deeply to me. It reminds me of the hands of my father and my paternal grandfather. My father's hands must be an exact reproduction of his father's. Their hands are very wide, with short thick fingers. By the time they reached middle age, their hands were roughened from all the water and hygienic soap their profession demands that they use. My father, like his father, is an orthodontist. His hands spend hours expertly bending small wires and wrestling metal bands onto teeth.

Yet his hands, which look so rough and worn, can accomplish the most delicate tasks. I remember watching my father wrap gifts. He could fold paper in a way that made it seem to have a life of its own, as it settled into beautiful patterns and perfect lines.

Lately, he has taken up weaving baskets and wreaths out of grapevines. His hands are his gift. They easily accomplish tasks which most of us would find frustrating or impossible.

It isn't just what those hands can accomplish that I remember, but also what they represented to me as a child. As we hiked the mountains near our home, we would often come to a precipice I was eager to look over. Sometimes we would come to ledges we needed to walk along to continue on the path. Then my father's arm would stretch out, offering the hand I could take to safely negotiate the steep places. I could trust those hands.

There came the tragic day my sixteen-year-old cousin, the youngest child of my father's brother, was killed in a train accident. When I went with my father to my uncle's home, he stretched out his hand to take mine as we walked up the driveway. The gesture didn't need words. It spoke of his love and his grief and the acknowledgment that life is not something we can easily walk through or understand.

But his hand was there for me to take, showing the way through shock and sorrow. His outstretched hand was a groaning beyond speaking, an act of solidarity with those struck dumb by grief.

When our youngest son, Daniel, was born, I looked down at his hands. There were the hands of my father and grandfather in tiny form. Those hands can already do things that require such coordination and strength. The hands of the fathers have been revealed in this little son, just as the outstretched hand of our God has been revealed in the Son, Jesus of Nazareth.

In Isaiah 53, the prophet asks, "To whom has the arm [and the hand] of the Lord been revealed?" The response is that the hand of the Lord had been revealed in the most unexpected way—in a child that would be born when the hope of Israel would seem dead.

This child would spring like a tender young shoot from a root in dry ground. The root would seem dead but would reveal life sustained deep within. The arm and hand of the Lord would be revealed in one whose appearance would not make people turn to him. He would not be dressed in a king's robes, with a crown on his head, so people would notice his authority.

No, his authority would come from serving. He would share our sickness, carry our sorrows. He himself would stretch out his arm and extend his hands in healing and love, in forgiveness and redemption.

And the arm of the Lord would be so powerfully revealed in him that he would finally be a threat to those who sought earthly power. Those arms, those hands, would be outstretched in the agony of crucifixion. Then his arms would gather us all into life everlasting, like a shepherd gathers in a flock of lost sheep.

Our Christ would have no natural descendants through whom his hands could be revealed. His life would be poured out without regard for securing his own lineage. Yet to him would God give innumerable descendants——more than the stars in the sky and the grains of sand on the shore.

We, the church of believers, are his children, through whom his outstretched arm and hand are now revealed. We are the lineage of Christ Jesus.

Our loved ones and church family became for us the outstretched arm and mighty hand of God, extended to us in deepest sorrow and grief. As Christ Jesus bore the insults and agony of this world, so our congregation bore our insults and sorrow. This changed our lives forever. It lifted us out of the depths into the light. It showed us the salvation of the Lord.

9

The day after Greg Robinson tried to break through our front door, Alberto asked our police precinct for help in mediating the situation. Alberto talked to a community liaison officer, but little came of it. The police had little authority and no programs with which to mediate a situation like ours.

One community liaison officer told us that all we could do was to press charges if we wanted continued support from the police. The police informed us that the charges of attempted assault from early Easter morning had been dropped by Stan's friend. Therefore, our charges were the only ones confronting Greg.

The charges did not mean Greg was in jail, however. He had been released on bond the morning of April 22, less than 12 hours after the incident. He would await his hearing while free to create other incidents.

A few nights later, we awoke to incredibly loud music blaring somewhere outside. We looked out the window. Greg's truck was parked across the street, with the stereo going full blast. Gary was slumped over the steering wheel. Alberto went down to our front porch, and, as he stood there, the lights at a nearby neighbor's home went on. Next Stan arrived home from work, pulled up in front of his house, and got out of his car. He and Alberto discussed what to do.

They were too intimidated by Greg to ask him to turn the stereo off. Alberto decided to call the police. The dispatcher informed him that a police squad was already on the way, presumably from an earlier call by someone else. The police arrived as Alberto was walking back outside. They convinced Greg to turn off the stereo and go inside his home.

But then Greg noticed Alberto. "I'm going to get you, neighbor. I'm going to get you!" Greg yelled.

Now Alberto and I began to discuss alternative ways to handle the escalating situation. We thought our neighbors, frightened by a number of incidents in addition to ours, might want to set up a neighborhood watch network. Neighbors would then agree to look out for each other. Alberto and I hoped that the Robinsons would attend and that organizing our block into a watch group would encourage them to supervise their teenagers more closely. We did not plan to confront them with the incidents involving Greg.

May came, turning our thoughts to our yard. All our young trees had survived the winter, and I was eager to add shrubs and plant a new garden. After the long Minnesota winter, May is always an exhilarating month—a time of fresh greenness and gentle warmth that clears winter out of mind and spirit.

Alberto began to work around the yard. He was digging up a new flower bed near our fence on a Saturday when John Robinson approached. There was still a gaping hole in the fence from the Easter trouble.

Suddenly, John screamed at Alberto, "What are you going to do about this fence?"

Alberto, startled, looked at John and replied, "The question is, 'What are *we* going to do about the fence?'"

John yelled, "Well, I don't need a fence. It's your stupid fence. If it was up to me, I'd get a saw and tear the whole thing down! Do you need a fence?"

Alberto's reply was quiet but contained rare anger. "I wouldn't need a fence if you'd keep your kids out of my yard."

"You've had your chance," John replied. "If I hear anything about this anymore, I'll beat you. Every time you walk out the door, I'll going to beat the s--- out of you!"

Alberto wearily interrupted the tirade. "John, I'm not interested in talking to you if you're going to stand there and threaten me."

John yelled, "I don't threaten! I *do*. And when I do, you're going to be in the hospital. You damn nigger!"

Now Greg showed up, and John stomped away. Greg looked at Alberto, and said, "You scum, you're giving us more trouble, aren't you?"

Greg walked away and Alberto continued to work dispiritedly. It was one of the last times I saw Alberto work in the yard except to quickly mow the grass.

On May 5, Greg was arraigned in court. He pleaded not guilty and a court date was set. He was released on the condition that "he not harass, annoy, injure, or have any contact with Alberto Quintela." Although we were unaware of Greg's arraignment date, we were informed by mail of the condition of his release.

May 6 was the date we had set for the first neighborhood meeting. Early in May, Alberto and I contacted each neighbor on our block. We asked them to attend a meeting at our home to discuss setting up a neighbor-hood watch network. We asked the neighbors across the street to invite Brenda and John Robinson.

Nine of our neighbors came to the meeting, but not the Robinsons. The police precinct sent an officer to tell us what to do if we saw anything or anyone suspi-cious in our neighborhood. He stressed that people looking out for one another is the best deterrent to neighborhood crime.

Recent incidents were discussed, including a smashed windshield, a prowler, and the noise from the Robinson property. Alberto and I tried to ensure that the comments didn't focus on the Robinsons.

Mrs. Brown mentioned that the Robinsons had been kind to her husband before he died and had supported her during his illness. Alberto and I suggested that anyone awakened in the night by anything suspicious turn on a porch light. The light would signal that this household could be summoned for help.

After the meeting, Alberto and I felt encouraged. We had talked to neighbors we did not know well. We hoped that we would receive support in seeking a peaceful, secure neighborhood.

Ten days later, on another Saturday afternoon, Al-berto, Joseph, and I were enjoying a picnic lunch in the backyard. Alberto had been cutting the grass, and I had been working in the garden. I decided to bring our lunch outside because it was such a beautiful day.

As we finished our meal, Greg Robinson appeared at our property line, where the fence gaped open. He pointed to himself and then to us, with a questioning look on his face. Still clinging to my hopes for a reconciliation with Greg and his family, I interpreted his motions to mean that he wanted to come over to us and apologize for past behavior. I told him that he could come into the yard.

Immediately, I sensed that I had entirely misjudged Greg's intentions. With a gasoline can in his hand, he knelt in front of us, and motioned toward me and Joseph, who was sitting up between Alberto and me.

"I don't have any argument with you," Greg flung in my direction. "I didn't come here to talk to you."

Then Greg looked over at Alberto and began to threaten him, saying, "But whoever puts me in jail, I'm going to knock their head off. You press charges, I'm going to knock your head off. You're a lawyer, so you think you're tough; if you're so tough, why don't you do something now that the police aren't here?"

"Go home, Greg!" I said firmly, panic rising. "Go home!"

Greg ignored me and began to yell obscenities at Alberto, "You scumbag lawyer! You think you can come here and run this place."

I sat rooted to the spot for a few seconds, as did Alberto, who was tightly controlling himself. He did not look at or speak to Greg. I realized we needed help. I decided, in those endless seconds, to get someone from the Robinson family to take Greg home.

I also decided to leave little Joseph sitting there beside Alberto. To get up and move away from the baby was agony, but I strongly sensed that Joseph's tiny presence might be the only thing that would keep Greg from attacking Alberto. *But what if Greg attacks Alberto and injures Joseph accidentally!* my mind screamed.

It was a horrifying decision, but I got up and ran toward the Robinson's home, knocking frantically and calling loudly for Brenda or John. No one came. I could hear Greg's voice getting louder.

Later, Alberto told me that Greg reached over and pushed him on the shoulder, grabbed his chin, and said, "Come on, fight. Let's fight. You wanna do something about it? Don't be a coward. Do it man to man. It's between you and me."

Alberto kept repeating, "Get off my property, Greg. I don't want you here. I don't want to fight. Go home!"

I finally gave up knocking on the Robinsons's door. As I was about to run back to our yard, a car drove up in the alley beside the Robinson's home and stopped. The young man driving the car said, "Where's Greg?"

I realized he thought I was Greg's sister. "He's in our backyard, threatening my husband," I said frantically.

The young man got out of his car and called to Greg. Thankfully, Greg responded. He picked up his gasoline can and walked back to his yard.

"Did you get gas for the mower?" we could hear the man asking Greg. They went into the garage, filled it, and drove off in the car.

We were left trembling. I picked up Joseph and held him close to my chest, talking to him softly. Alberto went inside the house. I could hear the typewriter going at a staccato pace. Later, Alberto brought me a letter he had written to John Robinson, informing him of this afternoon's incident with Greg.

In the letter, Alberto pointed out that Greg had violated his release condition. However, we would not press for court's action since I had invited Greg to come into our backyard. Alberto said that we would report any future incidents to the proper authorities. He sent copies of this letter to the judge who had arraigned Greg and to the prosecuting attorney.

Slowly the tension and fears of our encounters with Greg began to affect the patterns of our life. I began to watch for Alberto's return in the evenings after work. He rode the bus from his downtown office, then walked a few blocks to our house. I became fearful that Greg, and possibly his brothers or friends, would attack Alberto on the way home.

If Alberto was late coming home from work, I would feel unreasoning panic. If he took the car out at night for a meeting, I would wait up until he came in and watch him walk from the garage to our back door.

I quit going to meetings or get-togethers with friends at night. I wouldn't leave Alberto and Joseph alone in the house at night because I felt my presence might prevent an attack on Alberto. I became protective of my husband and child, irrationally believing that somehow I could stop whatever threatened them. If an attack ensued, I reasoned, the attacker must go through my body first. And so I watched and waited with quiet but determined dread.

Alberto stopped going into our backyard for anything but mowing the grass. He went to many evening meetings, and I wondered if he did this to avoid being home. I understood how he must feel, but I missed him when he was gone three or four nights a week. I clung to the fact that, in early June, we were leaving for two and a half weeks in South Carolina with my family. We desperately needed a break.

10

We left for South Carolina in June to spend time with my family. We were greatly relieved to be away. We shared the spring's events with my parents. However, once we were distant from the Robinson's abuse, we became more hopeful that their harassment would end as a result of the pending trial. We left my family, feeling refreshed and full of new hope for our lives in St. Paul. When we returned home, two to three weeks went by without incident. We told ourselves the situation was turning around.

It wasn't. Before I go on, let me explain the obscenities that are about to appear. Although the Robinsons constantly showered us with foul words, I have not shared them fully because this book would have been unpublishable in most Christian circles.

Here I must be frank. How can we as North American Christians ignore or escape the painful reality of the racial discrimination that continues to demean, deface, and abuse persons of color in our society? The experiences and abusive language recorded in the pages of this book are least among the experiences and epithets that most people of color encounter all the days of their lives. These sufferers are the ones for whom this story is told. They deserve for it to be recounted in all its horrible detail, even if that detail offends or shocks.

Furthermore, this story is told as a witness to the present reality of Jesus Christ, who himself suffered and died, abused and demeaned.

We confess that Jesus Christ is present when believers are gathered in his name. If this is truly so, the Jesus Christ who never flinched from the obscene realities of his day was present in our house on Baker Street. Jesus' own ears heard and bore the obscene language we lived with every day.

The incident that shattered our calm spanned the night of July 2 and early morning hours of July 3. Joseph and I had gone to bed. Alberto was watching television. It was near midnight. The Robinsons had been drinking since morning, and now there was a large gathering of young people in their screen house.

Everyone was talking and laughing loudly, occasionally singing "Happy Birthday" songs to Brenda. Alberto turned off the television and prepared to climb the stairs to bed. The sound of Greg's voice reached his ears above the rumblings of the party.

"Yeah, I was arrested," Greg was saying, "but I don't give a f--- about the neighbors or their baby. Let's party! He thinks he can control everything. I've been here about 16 years and he's only been here one year. Who does he think he is!"

Then, with chilling clarity, Alberto heard Brenda, seemingly the only adult in the gathering, yell, "Yeah, I don't give a f--- about those f---ing Mexicans!"

Alberto walked to the kitchen at the back of the house and looked out the window. There were Greg and some buddies lined up at the hole in the fence, urinating over into our yard while Greg urged them on with, "Let's piss all over them!"

After they finished, they went back to the screen house. In a few minutes, a round of choruses began. Brenda gave the count, "One, two, three," at which everyone yelled drunkenly, "F---ING MEXICANS!"

At the yelling in unison, I woke. I felt groggy, and couldn't tell whether I was dreaming or awake. The voices screaming outside my window had a nightmarish quality to them that I could not shake.

I got out of bed, trembling. For a few seconds, I wasn't sure where Alberto was. I started calling for him, running down the stairs, the chorus of voices rushing at me like demons in the night. I found Alberto at the downstairs phone, calling the police. But as in past incidents, someone had already called the station. Squad cars were on their way, sirens blasting into the night. Four or five police cars pulled up outside the Robinson household, and officers came walking resolutely toward the screen house.

They pounded on the screen house door, which apparently was locked. They warned that the party must immediately disperse or they would arrest everyone. They told Brenda that she was responsible for sending all the young people home. If she failed to end the disturbance, they would return to make arrests.

Quickly, many of the young people began to leave. Four or five went into the house with Greg, his brothers, and Brenda. The police left. For a short time, all was quiet.

We were just settling down to sleep when yelling

and cursing came rushing out of the Robinson's house. John had returned home, and he was sweeping the whole household back out to the screen house for a resumption of the party. Almost immediately, the police appeared again. We heard one officer say to John, "Sir, you are under arrest."

"Where's my gun? Where's my gun!' Greg screamed.

Alberto and I retreated toward Joseph's front bedroom, as far away from the windows that faced the Robinson's house as possible. Terrified, we wondered if this insane young man owned a firearm. The possibility had never occurred to us.

The next moments were a blur. All we could hear was screaming and yelling and commands by the police. We huddled in Joseph's room, listening.

Piecing it all together the next day from the accounts of neighbors who gathered out on the street, we learned that everyone in the house and screen house had indeed been arrested. John had resisted arrest, bashing his head through the window of a squad car. Brenda had been overcome by what she claimed was an asthma attack as they carried her to a waiting squad car. She had been taken away in a paramedic unit instead. Greg, his brothers, and several friends had all been arrested. The youngest child, a twelve-year-old, had been taken into protective custody by the police.

The nights that followed were sleepless. The Robinson family members appeared back home one by one, released as usual on bail. While they all seemed subdued in their public behavior, the tensions in their family were obviously mounting.

In the past month, two children who had been absent from the family for a long time had returned. One was the Robinson's daughter Rachael, who had threatened to jump from a second story window earlier in the fall. The other was the oldest son, who had been serving a sentence for theft. The daily cursing and shouting resumed. Rachael and Brenda fought constantly, as did Greg and his father.

On July 10, we had to appear in court for Greg's hearing on the April trespassing charges. Greg represented himself. He and a friend testified on his behalf. Then the city attorney called us to testify. The judge found Greg guilty and sentenced him to three months of attendance at Alcoholics Anonymous meetings. The judge also ordered Greg not to bother us in any way, and told us to contact him if any harassment occurred.

A few days later, the family members and friends arrested on public nuisance charges from July 2 and 3 were arraigned. Pleading guilty, Greg received a partially suspended fine and a three-day jail sentence.

We learned about Greg's jail sentence through a threat from his sister. I was returning home on my bicycle the evening of July 14, when I encountered Rachael.

She walked up to me, yelling obscenities about Alberto. "You know what I mean," she screamed, "You send Greg to jail, you'll see what happens."

I was initially confused. We had specifically asked the judge who heard the trespassing charges not to issue a jail sentence. We preferred to see Greg sentenced to chemical dependency treatment. Only later did I understand that Rachael was referring to Greg's jail sentence from the night of the July 2-3 party. We had not filed any charges in that situation. The police had declared the party a public nuisance.

But, like the rest of her family, Rachael viewed Alberto as responsible for all the trouble her family was experiencing. He had become their scapegoat. He was an attorney, part of the legal system which confronted their abusive and destructive behavior. In addition, he was a person of color, a person who "didn't know his place," who refused to acquiesce to their threats.

We were to pay dearly now for the charges we pressed against Greg and for the Robinson's perception that we were at the root of all their recent troubles. About a week after Greg served his jail sentence, we returned home from a long Sunday outing to find our kitchen window smashed. As we drove up beside our garage, I saw the jagged edges of the window facing our backyard.

My heart began to race. It was only late afternoon, the middle of a long hot still day. The first observation that hit me was that the neighborhood seemed as still as the day. There were no usual sounds of children playing, radios tuned to rock stations, or lawn mowers whirring. Where was everyone? Had no one heard the smashing of a window in the middle of the afternoon—on a block where everyone opened their houses up to the summer breezes?

In that moment, I understood fully what was happening. I knew that our neighbors had been tentative at the neighborhood watch meeting. I had to admit that through the whole spring and summer, no one had supported us in any overt way that might make them targets of the Robinson's wrath. We were, and would be, utterly alone. We were expendable in the long history of our neighbors' submission to the Robinson's abuse.

The silence of that afternoon, broken only by the flap of my kitchen curtain through the jagged glass of the window, spoke more loudly than words. The rock that was hurled through our window might as well have hit me in the chest. My breath was taken away by the realization that there was no one to help us.

Alberto remembers that I became hysterical. All I remember are vivid mental photographs of the kitchen and dining room of our home. I was aware only of the sensation of blood racing through my body, propelling me toward the house and the havoc that had been wrecked there.

When we entered the kitchen through the back door, I saw a large gash in the molding around the floor. Whatever had been hurled through the window had landed there with force. The brick or rock used to smash the window was nowhere in sight. It had obviously been removed. The faucet arm hung crazily down into the sink, broken off. There was dirt all over the kitchen floor.

I walked into the dining room. Here, someone had taken up the large china bowl given to us as a wedding gift and hurled it across the room, aiming at Joseph's wooden highchair. Its tray was deeply gashed and covered with blue pieces of china. The sugar bowl and salt and pepper shakers had been swept off the table and were scattered and cracked on the floor.

I ran through the rest of the house before I calmed

down enough to realize that the dining room and kitchen were the extent of the vandalism. Whoever had entered the house had been frightened of remaining too long.

Alberto was reaching for the phone to call the police. I stopped him. I was weeping and trying to tell him that it wouldn't do any good. It would just be a replay. We would call the police, they would come and file a report, we would press charges, and be left alone while the Robinsons worked their revenge. How could we live with such a cycle of fear and hatred?

"But what else can we do?" Alberto asked.

Our aloneness kept hitting me in waves of nauseating despair. I grasped at something that had never occurred to me or to Alberto before.

"Let me call Berry, please," I said, referring to one of our close friends from Faith Mennonite Church. "I want to ask him to come and help us. Then we'll call the police when he gets here. I just want someone with us."

I didn't know if I could go on. The terror and despair were overwhelming me. The violation of our home signaled just how far the Robinsons meant to go. In the past they had limited their violence largely to words. Now physical attack seemed probable.

Berry Friesen's voice on the phone helped calm the waves of nausea that were engulfing me. He was on his way, he said. I don't remember what I told him. But he arrived quickly and had Frank Trnka, another friend from the church, with him.

As they walked into our home, I saw shock and concern on their faces. It was the first time someone's reaction to our story or our plight seemed to match what I felt inside. These two brothers were seeing what we had seen. They were experiencing some of the shock we felt and the fear we had lived with for months. I was deeply grateful for their presence.

When they arrived, we called the police and went through the endless reporting any crime requires. While the police investigated the footprints leading from the garden under the kitchen window to the hole in the fence between our home and the Robinson's, the oldest Robinson son returned. He told the police no one had been home all afternoon. The police questioned the neighbors. Only one woman said she heard glass breaking around midafternoon, but she had assumed that someone had dropped something.

After the police left, Berry and Frank stayed with us for awhile. Finally, comforted by their presence and weary from the ordeal, we saw them to the door and climbed the stairs to bed.

11

After sharing our ordeal with Berry and Frank, we shared our fear more openly with other people. We realized that in the past months we had shared the facts of each incident with family and friends, but we had never shared how we felt as victims of this harassment and violence. We had not admitted our powerlessness and our fear. We had not talked about ways this victimization had changed the habits of our lives into patterns of desperate survival.

Most of all, we did not want to speak of our mounting anger and hatred for the Robinsons. We feared these feelings more than anything. They were like a rampant cancer within us. We knew with grim certainty that the time was coming when we would finally give nod to the folks who were ready to wreck vengeance on the Robinsons for us. We were a word away from the street war that would start when we uttered a simple "yes."

On the Tuesday evening after the break-in, Luis and Tules Aquilar came for our weekly home Bible study. Louis and Jules were a couple we had met through our community involvement. They attended a small Hispanic Pentecostal church, Tempo de Fe. They had a daughter just a little older than Joseph. We had been meeting for Bible study and prayer together during the summer while Joseph and Karina played happily around us.

That evening, we shared our mounting apprehension and despair with Tules and Luis. In the circle of their concern and response to us, a gentle wind began to blow through our hearts.

Alberto spoke softly of what it might take to bring us back from the edge of the abyss. He spoke of how redemptive it had been to experience Frank and Berry's response. He suggested that perhaps we needed our church family and close friends to stay in our home for a while. This might help us regain a sense of security in our house, reaffirm our nonviolent response to the Robinsons, and be a witness of Christian community to neighbors reluctant to become involved in our situation. Tules and Luis were willing to ask their pastor and church members to support us as well.

The four of us decided to ask the members of both Templo de Fe and Faith Mennonite Church, along with our close community friends, to meet in our home the Friday night following the break-in.

At this meeting, Alberto would share our story, and we would pray together. We would light candles as a symbol of peace. We would ask our friends to sign up to stay with us on shifts, 24 hours a day for seven days, in a vigil of peace and solidarity.

When Tules and Luis left, we felt great relief. It was as if we had crossed an enormous barrier. More accurately, it was as if the Holy Spirit had taken down the walls of silence and guilt. We would no longer hide what we were experiencing. The peace vigil would be, for us, a voice of protest and need.

For the next two days, Alberto and I contacted our friends. Some women from our church, who met for weekly meetings, were at our home on Wednesday morning and enthusiastically agreed to contact everyone at Faith Mennonite Church. Meanwhile, Tules and Luis were contacting members of their church.

More than thirty people crowded into our home on Friday night. Many more called to hear our story and to volunteer their time if we needed them to stay with us in the coming week. Alberto had written a brief account of our ordeal and had made copies of this and of police reports for people to read as they came in.

When everyone was seated around our living and dining room, Alberto began the painful recounting. At many points, his voice broke into weeping. For the first time, I fully realized what a terrible toll the months of our ordeal had taken.

Alberto recollected the language the Robinsons had used. This honesty had a profound effect on our friends, who had gathered to listen. The obscenities and racial epithets which the Robinsons had repeatedly used were as shocking and dehumanizing for our friends to hear as they had been for us. Alberto's recitation of the incidents we had been through, and the obscenities we had endured for months, created a vivid picture of the hell in which we had been living.

Finally Alberto explained our need for the constant presence of friends in our home over the coming week. "We have lost this home." he said. "We no longer feel safe here. Helen and I are asking you to help us regain our home—to help us feel at peace here again."

After Alberto's presentation, we prayed in English and in Spanish. Following the prayers, we each lit a candle to symbolize the beginning of the peace vigil. Then people signed up for shifts throughout the coming week. The shifts ran from 7:00 a.m. to noon, from noon to 4:00 p.m., from 4:00 to 11:00 p.m., and overnight from 11:00 to 7:00 the next morning. As people finished with the sign-up sheets, they expressed their support and commitment.

When everyone had left, we turned to each other, a hint of joy and hope in our faces. Someone would be back at 7:00 the next morning to begin the constant vigil. In reviewing the sign-up sheets, we discovered all but two spaces were filled, and many of the people who had called were ready to fill the remaining spaces. We were not alone!

The seven-day peace vigil was an experience of Christian response that will always live in us. It was much like an extended family experience. Mealtimes became communal gatherings of worship. We came to know church members and friends in a new way as we each shared feelings and past experiences.

Among other topics, we wrestled with the Christian response to violence. We discussed Jesus' teaching that we should love neighbors and enemies. We prayed together. We asked God for strength and guidance. We praised God for giving us this experience of communion in the midst of turmoil and fear.

I have many impressions of the week. I remember the blessedness of deep sleep after a long period of restless slumber. Each night when I went to bed, I knew there were people with us. Whatever happened, they would be with us. I enjoyed nights of dreamless sleep, uninterrupted by nightmares real or imagined.

I remember especially those people who brought their children. With sleeping bags and diaper bags slung over their shoulders, they were equipped to spend the night on our living room floor. They brought their children, their most precious gifts, into a house threatened by the forces of hell.

Nothing had haunted me as much as the thought of what might happen to Joseph if one of the Robinsons decided to enter our home while we were there. Most nights, he slept with us in our bed, where I could reach him the instant anything happened. I never left him for one minute out in his playpen in the yard.

My sisters and brothers in faith shared even these frightful, unspoken risks during the hours of their vigil in our home. Ultimately, we were powerless to protect our children from the evil unleashed on us. If there was one act that bound me forever to the church—to the gathered community of God's people—it was this foolish (as the world would see it) solidarity of my brothers and sisters. Risking everything, they stood with us in the darkness.

I remember that everything we did that week was penetrated by a sense of sacredness. Our supporters were with us in the name of the Lord. Laundry was washed and folded, meals were cooked and eaten, dishes were washed and bathrooms scrubbed in a light that was not extinguished by fear.

Many neighbors who saw all the people coming and going asked how I could stand having people constantly in our house. The question seemed absurd. My heart asked, "How could we stand it if they were *not* in our home?"

One morning in midweek, Berry Friesen's wife, Sharon, looked out our window at our car parked beside the garage.

"Helen," she exclaimed, "all the tires on your car are flat!"

I looked out the window, and felt her arms go around me. When we went out to look, we suspected they were slashed. We called a local auto-repair shop. The serviceman pumped air into the tires, then ran a brush with soap around the rims. The air swishing out, creating bubbles in the soap, revealed about eight small punctures along the side of each tire. He looked up and said, "Someone must not like you much!"

We called the police and made a report. The friend who came to us on the afternoon shift took me to buy four new tires. We never left the car out overnight again. Thus, four weeks later, it would be destroyed inside the ignited garage.

While the actual vigil lasted one week, it changed the way we responded in the weeks ahead. We no longer tried to manage the grief and stress alone. We sought help, not through guns or street vengeance, but through having our burdens shared in the frightful days to come. This support of our brothers and sisters in Christ let us respond peacefully to the Robinsons despite our mounting anger and hatred. No solution was in sight. No reconciliation seemed possible. Yet it seemed possible to endure the injustice as long as we were accompanied on the way.

John Howard Yoder, in his book *Nevertheless*, says

this about the communal necessity of a sustained non-violent witness:

> When we speak of the pacifism of the messianic *community*, we move the focus of ethical concern from the individual asking him[her]self about right and wrong in concern for his [her] own integrity, to the human community experiencing in its life a foretaste of God's kingdom. The pacifistic experience is communal in that it is not a life alone for heroic personalities but for a society. It is communal in that it is lived by a brotherhood of men and women who instruct one another, forgive one another, bear one another's burdens, reinforce one another's witness.

Yoder's words reflect our own experience. The violence directed at our family demanded a response, but maintaining a continued peaceful response on our own became impossible. Part of our powerlessness stemmed from realizing that we were not only powerless over the Robinson's actions, but also powerless over our mounting feelings of vengefulness.

The support of our Christian community turned these feelings of personal powerlessness into the power of a communal witness shared by all who gathered to risk violence and share injustice. We survived because our sisters and brothers in Christ took seriously the call to be the body of Christ in our home and surrounded us with Christ's peace.

12

Well'm, faith ain't no magic wand or money-back gar'ntee, either one. Hit's jest a way a-livin'. Hit means you don't worry th'ew the days. Hit means you go'n be holdin' on to God in good or bad times, and you accept whatever happens. Hit means you respect life like it is—like God made it—even when it ain't what you'd order from the wholesale house. Faith don't mean the Lord is go'n make lions lay down with lambs jest caus you ast him to, or make fire not burn. Some folks, when they pray to git well and don't even git better, they say God let'm down. But I say thet warn't even what Jesus was a-talkin' bout. When Jesus said ast and you'll git it, He was sayin' thet if'n you git beat down—scairt to death you cain't do what you got to, or scairt you go'n die, or scairt folks won't like you—why, all you got to do is put yore hand in God's and He'll lift you up.

—Rucker, in *Cold Sassy Tree*, on his deathbed

Finally prayer becomes a silence in the face of suffering and grief. All bargain deadlines have passed, all hopes are dead. Energy is concentrated on enduring each hour. To enter such pain voluntarily, to accompany one who suffers or grieves, is to give up one's voice. There is nothing important to say, no words of comfort that won't sound hollow, no words of hope that won't seem a mockery.

The silence is first experienced as the absence of God. It is a radical challenge to faith. Those who draw close to one who is suffering risk hearing, "My God, my God, why have you forsaken me?"

Even the one from Nazareth did not endure the cross alone. At his feet stood the mute women. Though overcome with their own grief and despair at this final defeat, they clung to his side. Such solidarity in the face of pain and loss is unimaginable. We read over the scene at the cross so quickly. We do not wish to enter such pain too deeply. So we avoid the only fitting response to such pain.

Yet if we can endure the silence and look on the afflicted, something inside us is slowly loosed and freed. Our limbs take on a life of their own. They reach out in mute longing to embrace the one who suffers.

Our hands reach for the hands of the stricken. Our eyes learn to gaze on affliction we never knew we could endure. Our senses come alive with awareness of the needs and the thoughts of the one to whom we have drawn close. Our throats utter wails of protest. Tears of living water stream down our faces. A part of us which we usually subdue comes alive.

We begin to hear the words of the Lord spoken to those no longer deafened by their need to speak, to act, to force solutions. The presence of Christ, embodied in the community of the faithful, becomes sufficient.

It is the only Word that speaks to the suffering in which we have become immersed. It is the Word become flesh, the incarnation of the love of our God in the hands and feet, the eyes and ears of sisters and brothers who have become the anointed of God.

A week after the peace vigil ended, on a Sunday evening, members of our church and Templo de Fe gathered in our backyard for a picnic and hymn sing. This gathering would be a reminder to us and our neighbors that there were people to share our plight.

As we finished eating and began to sing, John Robinson stormed out of his house and started his chain saw. Exhaust fumes from the saw filled our eyes and noses as we sat on blankets in our yard. We could see him clearly through the gap in the fence. His face radiated hardened fury. We could no longer hear each other speak or sing.

After about five minutes, we sensed he would keep the saw going. We wearily gathered the food, blankets, and babies, and walked to the front of the house. We still had to shout to hear one another. Finally, we gave up, laughing and shaking our heads. We joined hands silently and bent our heads in prayer. One by one, people left, Tules and Luis remaining with us.

My spirit had been buoyed in the past ten days by the spirits of my sisters and brothers. But as the hymn sing broke up and the noise of the chain saw wore on, I lost hope. The physical sickness and nausea I had experienced the night of the break-in returned. My head spun. Tules supported me gently into the house and up to bed. I closed my eyes to shut out the world. But Tules took my hand in hers, anchoring me to life through her fingers.

13

On August 12, three days after the picnic and attempted hymn sing in our backyard, Alberto had to leave town on business. We were anxious about being separated for even a short time, but I did not plan to be alone in the house. During the summer, we had rented our spare bedroom to a seminary student who was working long hours in a nearby bean factory.

Since Bernie worked nights and went home on weekends and holidays, he had not experienced most of the incidents with the Robinsons. However, he did not have to work on the night of the 12th and would be at home. I had also invited Ava, a close friend of mine, to spend the night. It was in her home that we had celebrated Passover the night before Easter.

After we had talked together for most of the evening, Ava settled down for the night on our couch in the living room. Bernie was already asleep in his room at the front of the house. I had put Joseph down in his crib earlier and crawled into my bed about 11:30.

I slept soundly, but was awakened suddenly right after midnight. I sat up in bed. I thought I smelled smoke. I looked out the back window of my bedroom toward the alley and garage but could see nothing unusual. We had used many candles during the peace vigil. Perhaps I had been dreaming, and the smell had been a part of the dream.

I crept down the steep back stairwell that led to the kitchen. Ava had left the light on in the bathroom downstairs. I saw her sleeping on the couch. Assured that everything was fine, I went back up to bed and dozed off.

Suddenly, I was sitting up in bed. The smell of smoke was unmistakable now. I heard a roaring sound coming through the window from the direction of the alley. I jumped to the window to see flames engulfing our garage.

I sprang into action. I switched on the lights, but nothing happened. I remembered that the garage lights were wired into the house circuits. The flames were so fierce I wondered if our house was in danger. Smoke was pouring through our open windows.

I ran down the back stairs, calling desperately for Ava. As she got up and ran to me, I pointed wordlessly to the back window. Ava and I stared at the fire, and in that moment, we also saw John Robinson. He was dousing his garage with water from a hose, not two feet from the fire that was consuming our garage.

"Get Joseph and Bernie," I cried to Ava. "Get out of the house now!"

Ava ran upstairs while I dialed 911 and stammered into the phone that we had a fire burning in our garage. The dispatcher told me that they had already received a call and were on their way. Ava appeared at the bottom of the stairs with Bernie, who held Joseph in his arms. Joseph was awake and crying.

I opened the closet near the front door and passed

out coats for us to throw over our nightclothes. Then we went out into the night.

The garage was a raging inferno. I remembered that the car was inside, filled with gasoline. At that thought, something snapped inside me. I ran to the houses of my neighbors, pounding on their doors, calling for them to get up because our garage was on fire. I irrationally saw our whole neighborhood going up in flames. It seemed to take the fire trucks forever to come.

Ava tried to calm me, but I was hysterical. In my worst imaginings, I had never thought of a fire. To watch the flames leaping off the roof of the garage and raging around the edges was excruciating. It seemed like such a final act of destruction. It endangered not only us but everyone who lived close by.

As people gathered, they began to ask the inevitable, "What happened?"

I began to insist to anyone who would listen that someone had set the fire. I was sure of this. The fire was intended to make us give up. Finally a woman who I did not know dared to walk up to me and take my hands in hers.

She looked straight into my eyes and said, "I had a fire in my home. And you must listen to me. You must calm down before you collapse. Believe me. You are safe. Your baby is safe. No one is hurt."

I looked into her eyes and saw her compassion. I recognized the truth of her words. My hands gripped hers and I breathed deeply, calming enough to stand with her until they put out the flames.

While the fire was still smoldering, a fireman asked

if I had the keys to the car. Without thinking, I dug into the pocket of Alberto's overcoat, which I had pulled on before leaving the house, and came up with his keys.

Alberto had looked all over the house for them in the days before he left for Kansas, frustrated at not finding them. Their accessibility at that moment probably prevented the gas tank on our car from exploding. The firefighters were able to drive the blackened vehicle out of the garage and away from the heat.

Another fireman stepped up to me to take down some information. I told him that I believed the fire had been set. He left to look over the scene of the fire, returning later to say there was evidence one corner had been doused with gasoline.

It was then that I realized the Robinson's home was completely dark. It was the only house on the block not ablaze with lights. Not even a half-hour before, Ava and I had seen John hosing down his garage. Where was he now?

I told the investigator briefly about the difficulties we had had with the Robinsons, and of seeing John dousing his garage. The investigator went back to inspect the site more carefully.

Ava, Bernie, and I, along with Joseph, went back into the house. A neighbor, a young father from across the street, asked what he could do for us. The couple who lived next to him were also greatly concerned. It was the first time anyone had openly showed shock or concern over our situation.

The total destruction of our garage, car, and belongings had finally burned through our neighbors' apathy. No one had thought it would go this far. Now that we had all been endangered by the roaring flames of arson, our neighbors were willing to acknowledge that we needed their help. But their help came late.

No one in our household slept the rest of the night. The man from across the street sat up with us. I waited until early morning to call Alberto in Kansas. We both had become so exhausted by the long ordeal that I did not want to rob him of another night's rest. He would need his energy to deal long-distance with the discernment of what should be our next step.

For myself, I resolved that night that we would leave. I did not want to live in this house any longer. I did not want to wonder what would be next. If the next incident was worse than a fire in our garage, it would surely mean physical harm to one or all of us. No one could convince me to stay.

At 6:00 in the morning I placed the call to Alberto's hotel room. He groggily answered, and I told him as calmly as I could what had happened.

"What do you want me to do?" he asked.

"I want you to come home!" I nearly screamed. "I want to leave this place. I am *sick* of being afraid."

Unreasoning anger boiled up inside me. Why wasn't he here? And why didn't he say he would be home on the next plane? I tried to get control of my mounting rage.

"I'm going to hang up," I explained very slowly. "Why don't you go talk to Richard [Alberto's close friend who was there with him] and call me back in a little while?"

I hung up, shaking. I knew we were at the end of all our resources, emotionally, financially, and physically.

I picked the phone back up and dialed my parents in South Carolina. My father answered the phone with grogginess that echoed Alberto's. I started to speak, but was hardly able to stammer out my name.

He came instantly awake. "Sis!" he said, using my familial nickname.

I told him about the fire.

"We're coming," he replied. "Our suitcases are packed. We were leaving today for the beach. We can get there by tomorrow, early in the afternoon. Can you hang on that long?"

I assured him I could, that I had many people with me.

"Papa," I said, before we hung up. "I just want to get out of here. Will you help me? I can't live here any longer."

"As soon as I'm there, we'll find you a place," my father assured me.

I hung on to those words while enduring the hours it would take for my parents to arrive.

A few minutes later, our doorbell started to ring. From his hotel in Kansas, Alberto had called several Hispanic friends in our community, and they all burst onto the scene. Ava and Bernie spent the next hour cooking breakfast for the eight to ten people who showed up between 6:30 and 7:30 a.m.

Tules and Luis came. Frank Rodriguez, the state representative from our district, arrived. With him were other folks determined to take this case to the mayor, city council, the state human rights department, anyone who would *do* something. Most were outraged. I was too exhausted to care. I was leaving. That was the only meaningful response I could imagine.

I looked at Ava and knew she felt as I did. I walked over to her amid all the men arguing at our dining table about what should be done. I put my arms around her and begged her to go home and rest. She reluctantly agreed.

I walked into the study and called Ernie Miller, a church friend who was not teaching during the summer. I asked him to come stay with me for the day. I knew it was going to be hopelessly long. He said he would bring his daughter to help care for Joseph.

After about an hour, the folks who had come to survey the damage and determine what should be done left to begin the process of protest at the city level. Tules and Luis left to go to work. I called the insurance company, who would send an adjuster out later in the day. Ernie and his daughter arrived. Several neighbors stopped in with food.

Ernie and I, along with his daughter and Joseph, were eating lunch when a man burst through our front door. He was a small wiry man I did not know, but his actions seemed entirely appropriate in the middle of such a nightmare. I looked up calmly, wondering who he was and why he was in my living room.

"I want you to know, ma'am, that we are going to take care of this thing. We're ready to fight fire with fire. You don't have to do a thing. We'll do it for you."

"Do what?" I wanted to know.

"Take care of the Robinsons. Fight fire with fire."

The scene was insane. I felt light-headed, as if part of me was leaving already. I tried to focus on this man in front of me pacing agitatedly back and forth across the room. I felt a strange compassion for him. He seemed more upset than I.

"Would you like to sit down?" I asked.

"No ma'am, I've just come here to tell you we'll take care of it"

"Well, I appreciate your concern for us," I began. "But, you know, we don't have to live with the Robinsons forever. We do have to live with ourselves. If you and your friends hurt the Robinsons, we'll have to live with that knowledge for the rest of our lives. I'm going to ask you to go home. Let us handle it in the way we believe it should be handled. We have tried to respond to them peaceably, and we want to keep it that way."

"Okay," he said, "but you let me know. It can be done anytime you change you mind." And he was gone.

Alberto spent an equally nightmarish day in Kansas. Because of an air controller's strike, flights had been cut to a minimum, and he could not get an earlier ticket home. He would have to remain in Kansas until his scheduled departure date on Sunday.

He not only called his Hispanic friends who might have some influence to intercede in our situation, but also the police—whom he asked for round-the-clock protection for us until we could move.

This was impossible, the police insisted. But they did have off-duty police officers we could hire to guard the house at night. When Alberto called back later to make the final arrangements for such protection, they told him they were having trouble finding willing officers.

Most were familiar with the Robinsons. The police,

in fact, considered intervention at that residence very dangerous. The off-duty men were only willing to help us in teams of two. This meant twice the expense.

Someone from our church came to spend the night. I don't remember who it was. Many people would stay with us over the next week whose faces I cannot recall. I do not have images of those days as I do from the earlier days of the peace vigil.

I moved around in numb resignation. Eleanor and Perry Beachey came on Friday morning to stay until my parents arrived . They had stayed with us during the peace vigil as well. A couple close about my parents' age, they had spent the past few years caring for Perry's father, who had recently died. They were planning to enroll in the Mennonite seminary together, then accept a joint pastorate. Eleanor's quiet supportive manner had been a rock to me in the past months. I felt her calm creep into my own heart during the hours she spent with me.

My mother and father arrived shortly after lunch. I was upstairs lying down when I heard their voices. I ran down the stairs and into the shelter of their embrace.

My father walked out to the garage site and came back in. "Tomorrow, we'll go look at some apartments," he said grimly.

Not a word was said about how we could afford an apartment on top of house payments. His first concern, as was mine, was to get us out. He could stay until Sunday, when he would fly back home to work. My mother planned to stay as long as possible.

They had brought us their car, which they had

planned to sell soon. This was a wonderful gift. It solved our immediate need for an automobile, and we could reimburse them with the insurance settlement for our burned car.

Such financial concerns were only the beginning of expenses and financial losses that would almost bankrupt us. From the day after the fire, our debts would far exceed our income. Our monetary situation would become a source of new tension and unbearable stress in the year after our move from Baker Street.

Right now, financial concerns were the least of our worries. Dad and I started out next morning with the Saturday listings to find an apartment. We came home late that evening deeply discouraged. The places we could afford were dirty and dingy. Others accepted pets, but not children. Was there any place out there for us? Our search on Sunday yielded nothing. It was close to September and the beginning of the school year; most landlords had ten applicants for their units.

Dad had to catch his flight home Sunday afternoon. Leaving without knowing where we would live and what we would do must have been very painful for him. Shortly after I saw Dad off, Alberto arrived on a flight from Kansas. He, too, had decided we must move. I reported our fruitless search. We went to sleep that night wishing we could wake in a different world.

14

I know that I want to have a door in the depths of my being, a door that is not locked against the faces of all other
human beings. I know that I want to be able to say, from
those depths, "Naturally, come in, and come in."
Philip Hallie, *Lest Innocent Blood Be Shed*

The next day, on Monday, I went to the office of a
friend who had participated in the peace vigil and was
a realtor on the West Side. I told him I had not found
any place for us to live. He had just been speaking to a
man about a duplex unit for rent.

"Come on," he said, "we'll go take a look."

We pulled up to a big brick double home on a major
West Side street, about 10 blocks from the Baker Street
house. As we walked up the steps to the front of the
house, a voice above our heads called out a welcome.

I looked up to see a woman standing on the porch
roof, painting the second floor windows. Her face was
cheerful. I involuntarily smiled in return.

She introduced herself as Michelle. "Come in, come
in," she said, leading us to the side of the double home
that was for rent.

It was beautifully restored. She had done much of
the work herself. She and her family lived in the other

side of the house. They were asking a reasonable rent, and the unit was available the first of September. I took a deep breath and explained why we needed to move.

Michelle had a family, as we did. I felt she should know we were fleeing a violent and destructive situation over which we had no control. Michelle had about ten applicants for the unit, but after hearing my explanation, she said she would hold them until we could give her credit references.

Michelle and her family were Jehovah's Witnesses. Her response has made me unable, ever since, to turn one of her brothers or sisters in faith away. I remember what it meant to have her take us in even when we were not certain we would be free of the Robinsons's harassment. She extended refuge. The least I can do now is offer coffee and respect to those who drop by to talk about their understanding of faithfulness to God.

I brought Alberto over later in the day to see the duplex. We put down the damage deposit to secure the unit. Then we went home to arrange for the movers to pack up our household on Baker. My mother had insisted we let her hire the movers to get us out of the house. She sensed that the stress of packing and moving would break us emotionally and physically.

The moving company promised they could pack our belongings on Wednesday and have everything moved by Thursday. They would store our things in a warehouse for two weeks, until the rental unit became available.

The movers came early on Wednesday. My mother, Joseph, and I were going out to Chaska. There Joseph and I would spend the two weeks with our friends, the

Shermocks. Alberto had secured a room downtown so that he could work and finalize arrangements for our house on Baker.

We had decided to rebuild the garage and to rent the house. We wanted to honor our financial obligations for the property. We knew a foreclosure could mean not being able to purchase a home again for many years. Yet we were hesitant to rent or sell the house to anyone. We finally resolved that we would tell serious prospective renters and buyers why we had left. We didn't know any other way to live with ourselves.

My mother stayed in Chaska with Joseph and me for a week. She and Linda Shermock recall that I sat all day on Linda's couch, doing needlework and staring into space.

I remember little of that time. I was numb with shock and grief. I had been nursing Joseph, but my milk dried up a few days after the fire. My mother and Linda cared for Joseph. I could not respond even to him.

Joseph's first birthday came while we were at the Shermock's home. Alberto traveled out to Chaska that evening after work. Jim and Linda's anniversary was the same day, but they stayed home with us. Linda cooked a special meal and a cake for Joseph. She gave him a stick horse which he dragged happily along the floor as he crawled around the house. Yet I felt detached from everyone. I was filled with a sadness that allowed no joy. The day following Joseph's birthday was Alberto's thirtieth birthday, but I don't remember celebrating it at all.

Finally the day came to move into the rental unit. As

the movers brought in our things and began setting up the furniture, I revived enough to begin unpacking and sorting our belongings. The movers had made the transition far easier than I imagined it could be. Not one thing was broken or lost.

The second day in our new home, I stood by our bed, sorting out Joseph's clothes. I wondered if we could possibly put our shattered lives back together.

Just then I turned to look at Joseph, who had called out "Mama!" from the hallway. He was clinging to the wall, tottering on unsteady little legs. Suddenly he let go of the wall, and with a smile wreathing his face, took his first steps toward my arms.

For a long time after our move from Baker Street, Joseph was the only reason I made the effort to go on. I got out of bed each morning because he needed me, and I reached out to other people because he was such a sociable child.

Alberto and I, however, began to experience conflict. He had made the decision, in the two weeks Joseph and I were in Chaska and he was living downtown, to quit his job and go into private practice.

Years later, I would learn that this desire for change is a normal reaction to loss and grief. Grief counselors discourage major life-changes in the year following a significant loss.

Looking back, I realize that Alberto's work environment was probably a painful reminder of our lives on Baker Street. He always had to leave the house after a bad incident and go to his job. There, I imagine, he tried hopelessly to cope with the growing nightmare at home and the demands of work.

It is not surprising that his first reaction was to get out of this job at the same time that we left the house. I agreed to the change in my numbed state. Nothing seemed important to me anyway.

The leap into private practice greatly increased our financial burdens. Now we were in debt not only because of the Baker Street house but because of Alberto's practice. We took out a loan.

Shortly after the fire and the move to our new home, Alberto and I visited the state commissioner of human rights. We wanted to find out if the state would consider filing a human rights suit on our behalf.

The commissioner spent a long time with us. She said that if we had been renters of the Baker Street property, or if the Robinsons were renters, the state could file a discrimination suit. But because both parties were homeowners, any case filed would have to be a civil suit, initiated by us. She encouraged us to consider filing such a lawsuit.

Taking responsibility for a civil suit meant making ourselves vulnerable again to the Robinson's anger and revenge. I did not want this. Yet Alberto insisted that unless we pursued some form of legal action, such incidents could happen again and again. They could be instigated by the Robinsons or anyone else on the West Side who learned that it paid to harass minority peoples. Reluctantly I agreed. The human rights commissioner referred us to an attorney with legal experience in civil rights from the '60s.

Alberto felt strongly that we must remain on the West Side and somehow witness to the nonviolent resolution of conflict. I thought this was a wild dream. I became angry at Alberto. I was angry, too, about piling debt from his practice on top of the debt we already had. He avoided looking at our month-to-month finances, and I began to constantly bring up the subject.

I took Joseph home with me to South Carolina in November to visit my family. I was relieved to get away from our problems. But when I returned a week later, Alberto was in a frightening state. He was having mental blackouts. He would suddenly find himself driving past the Robinson's home. One day, he had opened the trunk of our car to find his hunting rifle there. He didn't remember putting it in the car. His state shocked me into calling a counseling center, and I made an appointment for us the following day.

Our session with the counselor was somewhat reassuring. He said there were analogies between what we had experienced on Baker Street and living in a combat zone. He explained that people surrounded by violence develop patterns of behavior to help cope with the threats. These are patterns of survival, but when one leaves the combat zone, the survival patterns can become self-destructive and also hurt relationships.

We returned over the next few months to the counselor, but finally ended the sessions in midwinter. We could no longer afford the expense.

15

How can I describe the darkness we lived in the year after the fire? We thought we could rebuild our lives. But evil is powerful. It reshapes lives into unhealthy, unlovely patterns. Our counselor's imagery of war zone habits imposed on peacetime existence is a psychological description of how evil affects those over whom it has thrown its cloak.

In *The Nature and Destiny of Man,* Reinhold Niebuhr describes evil as falsely interpreting the human condition and the nature of God. Niebuhr's interpretation underscores evil as ultimately deceptive. The Deceiver tells lies about who we are as human beings and who God is. I believe evil's ultimate lie about God is that "God is not here." The sufferer experiences this lie as truth. The sufferer is tempted to believe salvation will have to come from human effort.

Even in this temptation, the sufferer has a companion in Jesus of Nazareth. The ministry of Jesus is recorded as beginning with his baptism, followed by a long period—forty days and forty nights—of temptation. The Gospel of Matthew says that Jesus saw the Spirit of God descend upon him at his baptism. Jesus heard the voice of God, claiming him as a child with whom God was well pleased. The Gospel writer also remembers that the Spirit of God accompanied Jesus into the wilderness. "Then Jesus was led by the Spirit into the desert to be tempted by the devil" (Matt. 4:1).

Until recently, I had not noticed those words. I thought Jesus went alone into the desert with the Tempter. But the Gospel writer does not let us forget that God went and joined Jesus in that desert struggle.

This text has often been interpreted to mean that God led Jesus into the desert, as one would lead a lamb to the slaughter. I cannot understand such an interpretation. I believe the text means that God led Jesus as a Parent leads a child.

God was with Jesus even in the midst of his struggle with the Tempter, just as we draw closest to our children when they are struggling with sickness, failure, or even death. Where else would we be, except at their side, struggling with and for them? And if we, who are human, struggle with and for our children, how much more must God struggle on behalf of God's own children? Thus I believe that the Spirit of the living God hovered over Jesus throughout his struggle with the great Tempter.

What did the Tempter want? I think the Tempter wanted nothing more than for Jesus to claim he could save himself. The Tempter says (my paraphrase, here and in the following dialogue), "Turn these stones to bread if you are God's Son. Feed yourself." Jesus says he lives only by the bread God provides.

Then the Tempter says, "Throw yourself off this high place. Save yourself (or kill yourself)."

Jesus says, "My life is not mine to save or do away with. My life belongs to God. I will not test God."

Finally the great Tempter says, "Worship me—and all the earth will be yours."

But Jesus replies, "This earth doesn't belong to you or to me. You cannot give it and you cannot take it away. This earth can only be saved by the one who created it, whom I choose this day to worship."

Consider what Jesus is saying. "I cannot feed myself. I cannot save myself. I cannot save this world *without God*." Faced with this truth, the Tempter leaves Jesus in the company of angels and the Spirit of his God.

Jesus was struggling with the Tempter over who he was as the image of God, and over who God, the Creator, is. The Tempter wanted Jesus to accept the delusion that he could save himself.

We struggle with the same Tempter and delusion. At the root of our temptation is our anxiety over the finiteness of our lives. We worry about food, security, our lives, and our children's lives.

But Jesus asks, "Who of you by worrying can add a single hour to his [her] life?" (Matt. 6: 27). We read these words and know that to stop worrying is impossible for us. Yet Jesus was pointing to the source of our sin—the sin that leads us to believe we can or must save ourselves without God.

And if we can do without God, we can just do without the companionship and solidarity of our brothers and sisters in faith. Thus we begin to isolate ourselves from the body of Christ, from the flesh through which God makes evident our salvation.

Jesus himself gathered around him a community of faithful brothers and sisters—Peter and Andrew, Mary and Martha, Mary of Magdala and Joanna, James and

John. He did not try to suffer the consequences of faithfulness outside the saving presence and solidarity of people God called into being.

Thus Jesus' ministry echoed the promise made to Abraham and Sarah, "All peoples on earth will be blessed [saved] through you" (Gen. 12:3b). The ministry of Jesus Christ was one of reconciliation. This reconciliation between us and God is made evident as God's people gather to share burdens and joys. The mark of the early church Acts 2 was that the believers were *together*. They shared possessions and ate together with glad and sincere hearts.

Often the sufferer withdraws from human community and comfort. Perhaps this signifies the very rejection of God. For me, the year following the fire was one not only of physical, emotional, and marital crisis, but of faith crisis as well. My life had fallen apart. All the desires of my heart had been shattered. I clung to memories of the peace vigil, when we experienced the peace of Christ's body in the midst of violence.

Yet the assurance of God's presence in my suffering slowly seeped away. Alberto and I began to focus on each other and ourselves the anger we felt toward the Robinsons. I became furious with God. How could an almighty God have allowed this? Where was God as we fell apart, crushed by mounting debts, fear of retaliation from the lawsuit, and inability to understand or minister to one another?

I yielded to the Tempter's deception. I believed God had abandoned us. "So," I cried furiously to God, "if you will not save us, I will at least try."

I set out with grim determination. That spring I began to apply for work. As summer neared, I substituted for two weeks at a nearby school, then took two jobs. One was a secretarial job with the Hispanic Chamber of Commerce. The other was an on-call job that took me into the homes of elderly folks to cook and to do household chores. I also filled out applications for teaching positions in the fall.

I worked with a vengeance, juggling work schedules and care for Joseph. And I made another decision. I would not have more children. I did not want to bring another child into this grim world. No other child would see a first birthday pass with mourning and grief-stricken numbness. I told myself I was making this decision for Joseph's sake. The responsibility of guiding and raising only one child in such a sin-sick world made me despair.

The hours that both Alberto and I spent at work, caring for Joseph, and attending to the endless details of filing the lawsuit left us little time for each other. Because of our mounting despair and rage, we had little desire to be together anyway. By late spring, we were two adults living under the same roof, sharing only the bond of fierce love and protectiveness for our child. We fought often and bitterly.

I occasionally considered what it might be like to take Joseph and leave Alberto. The one thing that stopped me was seeing how much Joseph loved his father. I could not bring myself to hurt my child by abandoning my marriage. I hung on, with a wait-and-see attitude. I entered that summer of 1982 poised like a wounded deer for final flight.

16

Early in June 1982, our lawyer mailed us a copy of the lawsuit which he and his associates had been preparing for months. He included a letter telling us he was ready to file the suit whenever we were ready.

It arrived when Alberto was at a church event. I opened it and skimmed over the legal complaints. My reaction was physical as well as emotional. All the old fear and uncertainty arose. I began to shake. I wanted to run from this responsibility as much as I had wanted many, many times to run away from the Robinsons.

I asked myself again why we should file the suit and live again with the potentially violent behavior of the Robinsons. I doubted the Robinsons knew where we were living, but I was sure they could find us if they really wanted to. Alberto was too prominently involved in the West Side community to remain hidden from someone who wanted to harm him.

We kept our copy of the lawsuit for three or four weeks before acting. During those weeks, we truly talked for the first time in two or three months. We both knew that proceeding with the lawsuit would change our lives as irrevocably as had our victimization by the Robinsons. We knew we must be prepared for the changes and let God speak to our hearts during this new crisis.

This time of uncertainty drew us more closely together. We knew how to relate to one another in a critical situation. The old crisis patterns asserted themselves. I responded with great protectiveness toward Alberto and Joseph. Alberto made the final decision regarding the lawsuit. These old patterns felt comfortable, like worn garments. Our conflict and anger toward one another diminished for a short time.

The lawsuit asked for monetary retribution for property damages and for emotional suffering. After our experience on Baker, Alberto and I felt strongly that an offender must be nonviolently confronted by his or her victim in a safe setting. We believed an offender must be confronted with the victim's emotional struggle to live on with the losses and fears that accompany any victimization.

We knew that the Mennonite Church was involved in Victim-Offender Reconciliation programs in some areas. Victim-offender reconciliation programs see peaceful confrontation as vital to bringing new life and hope to both victim and offender.

Alberto and I felt we had tried to confront the Robinsons peacefully. We had attempted first to confront the Robinsons alone. Then we had tried a neighborhood meeting. Finally we worked through various agencies, such as the Crime-Victim Center, the department of Human Rights, and a police liaison officer.

No attempt had been successful. We believed that the civil court system should be a final resort for nonviolent conflict resolution and administration of justice. The Robinsons needed to be confronted with our losses. We prayed this would lead them to seek the professional and spiritual help they so desperately needed. We recognized that we greatly needed this justice to adjust to the changes and losses in our lives.

Our lawsuit was a public statement on various levels. First, it was a public affirmation of our belief in nonviolent conflict resolution. Second, it would serve notice on individuals who oppress others—due to their beliefs, ethnicity, or background—that the justice system would not condone such behavior. Third, we hoped it would empower other families and individuals similarly abused.

We especially hoped that the legal action would empower the Hispanic community in which we lived. Alberto and I shared concern with other individuals on the West Side over a rising wave of anti-racial and anti-ethnic unrest in our urban communities. We hoped actions such as ours would restore a measure of self-worth and reassurance in our divided neighborhoods.

In the final week of our discussions and soul-searching, a letter to the editor appeared in our local West Side paper, *The Voice*. The letter helped resolve our mixed feelings about the lawsuit. It was written by a former neighbor of a Hmong family who had been forced to move from their home in our community because of behavior similar to that of the Robinsons. The writer of the letter was outraged that this incident could happen in our community.

Reading the letter affirmed our decision to file our suit and seek justice for ourselves and others like this family. We hoped our West Side community and other multiethnic communities would see the need for community level groups to negotiate neighborhood disputes at an early stage, averting tragedies.

Alberto informed our attorney that we were ready to file the lawsuit. But we realized we would not be able to endure the consequences of the lawsuit alone. So we informed our friends and church family of our decision.

Alberto developed the idea of a group meeting at our church, during which we could explain how and why we had filed the suit. Alberto wrote a letter to our friends and church family. In it he explained the situation and asked people to meet on July 11, at Faith Mennonite Church. The purpose would be to discuss potential ramifications of filing the lawsuit and to plan for specific actions friends could take if a crisis arose. Our attorney and his associate agreed to be present and speak to the group.

Meanwhile, about a week before the meeting, Bernie Boyle, the student who had lived with us during the summer of 1981, called. Could he live with us for six weeks while he worked with Catholic Charities in St. Paul?

He said to Alberto, "I know you have so much on your minds now. My presence may be the last thing you need, but God has been speaking to me and telling me I should call."

We were, of course, overjoyed. We did need Bernie's presence. He would share our burden and lighten our load in the days to come. He had shared the terror of the night of the arson fire. More than anyone else, he could understand our feelings. We invited him to stay as long as he needed a place to live.

About thirty-five people gathered at Faith Mennonite for the July 11 meeting. Alberto began the meeting by restating our commitment to nonviolent confrontation of the Robinsons.

Next Myron Schrag, our pastor, spoke on the biblical principles of nonviolence and on our ministry to the city. He quoted Jeremiah 29:7, which calls the exiled people to "seek the peace and prosperity of the city to which I have carried you."

He referred to Matthew 5: 14-16:

> You are the light of the world. A city on a hill cannot be hidden. Neither do people light a lamp and put it under a bowl. Instead they put it on its stand, and it gives light to everyone in the house. In the same way, let your light shine before [all], that they may see your good deeds and praise your Father in heaven.

Myron also reviewed Christ's teachings concerning a brother or sister who sins against you. The steps for reconciliation from Matthew 18:15-20 are ones Alberto and I truly believed we had tried to follow with the Robinsons.

The text speaks of a brother (or sister) who sins against you. Throughout our ordeal and into this summer of '82, Alberto and I struggled to view the Robinsons as our brothers and sisters in God's eyes. We knew that the Creator cared for the Robinsons as much as for us, and that we were to deal with them as children of God. Our lawsuit was the final step in trying to confront them with their responsibilities as persons created in God's image.

Next our attorney spoke of his experiences in an Illinois town during the early '70s. He had been part of a team of lawyers that pursued civil and human rights through the federal court system on behalf of people in a town torn by regular shootings caused by racial hatreds. Our attorney stated his commitment to the courts as an avenue for justice.

We were all certainly concerned that the lawsuit would stir the Robinsons to violence. For Alberto and myself, there were issues of emotional and physical safety. For our church community, as for any pacifist community, there was the question of whether an action that might invite violent retaliation was proper. Alberto and I had discussed this concern at length. Finally, however, we stood on the model of the civil rights and United Farmworkers movements.

Both movements sought justice for the oppressed. Both were founded on the gospel ethic of love for enemy as well as neighbor. Yet these movements recognized the gospel imperative for justice and mercy. They did not seek to control reactions to the movements, but to keep the movements as faithful as humanly possible to the gospel of peace in Jesus Christ.

Such movements recognized that the ministry of Jesus of Nazareth and the early church triggered violent responses in those confronted. As the apostle Paul would later observe, the gospel is offensive to those who cannot hear its message.

The early Anabaptists understood this only too well. Thousands lost their lives in the wave of persecution that broke out against them when they stood upon the ground of the faithful. Yet they did not cease to stand because of the violence their radical faithfulness unleashed.

According to this view of peace and justice, peace is more than the absence of violence. It owns the Old Testament promise of *shalom*—of a time when all will be fed, when each will sit under her vineyard, when strife will cease and God's people will dwell together in peace, acknowledging the gifts of the Creator. The hope of this day includes not only the absence of enmity, but the presence of God's justice.

During the discussion that followed our attorney's presentation, it was evident that many of our church members, as we had anticipated, had questions and concerns. Mennonites have traditionally avoided using the courts.

Their reluctance is based on sound doctrine. As Alberto and I had tried to do, most Mennonites take the teachings of Matthew 18 seriously. They have traditionally settled disputes through following the prescribed order in Scripture. Reconciliation is first attempted one-to-one. If reconciliation is not possible on that level, a third person or persons are asked to be witnesses and to help negotiate a reconciliation. Finally, unresolved disputes are taken before the congregation.

Mennonites historically came from rural communities, where they lived among fellow Mennonites or people who shared the Christian tradition. Thus confrontation with a brother or sister had been successful in cases where both parties agreed on the binding nature of the biblical prescription and the authority of the Christian community. Mennonites who would not accept accountability to the church were loosed from the congregation and often drifted away.

Mennonites in urban areas or in areas where there is not a Mennonite community often experience broken relationships which cannot be resolved through the church. If both parties are not willing to accept the biblical prescription or the church's authority, the dispute cannot be resolved within the Christian community. It may become necessary for other institutions to help provide justice and reconciliation.

The July 11 meeting ended at 11:00 p.m., after four hours, and concluded on an uncertain note. Many of our brothers and sisters were not convinced the lawsuit was the best nonviolent alternative. Many discussed the possibility of visiting or writing letters to the Robinsons. Alberto felt it was too late for this.

The week following the meeting was especially hard for Alberto. We knew many members of our church family might have doubts about our legal action. But Alberto was discouraged by what he viewed as a lack of support. I strongly felt that some members of our church family were expressing doubts only about our legal actions, not about whether they would support us and love us once we made the final decision.

Myron, our pastor, came to see Alberto later in the week. Myron felt our actions were based on sound discernment of Christ's teachings. He felt that some people in the congregation simply needed time to consider our action of filing the lawsuit. Any doubt or disagreement over methods would make no difference in our church family's love and concern for us.

My greatest struggle during this period of discernment was to overcome my fear for Alberto's safety once the lawsuit was filed.

People often asked, "Aren't you afraid of what the Robinson's might do if you file this lawsuit?"

I was afraid. I prayed daily to have the strength to live with the fear. One night, early in July, I sat on our back porch reading John Perkins' book, *Let Justice Roll Down*. Perkins' account of his personal struggles and sacrifices in the civil rights movement had given me much encouragement and support that summer.

That night, as I read, I became aware of a stillness greater than the stillness of the hot summer evening. I listened to the profound quiet stealing over me in a soft wave of blessing. I could not remember feeling so emptied of worry and anxiety in a long time.

In that stillness, a thought brushed my mind. It was as if someone had painted a watercolor impression in my head. In another month, on August 7, Alberto and I would enter our seventh year of marriage, a sabbatical year. The words of Leviticus 25 spoke to me.

> But in the seventh year the land is to have a sabbath of rest, a sabbath to the Lord. Do not sow your fields or prune your vineyards. Do not reap what grows of itself or harvest the grapes of your untended vines. The land is to have a year of rest.

Could it be that Alberto and I would be given the peace and rest we so desperately needed? I did not understand how it could be accomplished, but I felt immeasurably comforted by this reassuring stillness. It was like a benediction. In the coming weeks, I would need the benediction to take me through the fear of death and into the shalom of a profound grace.

17

Looking back on those last days of July 1982, I see the outstretched hand of God. Strength and love was provided even before the time of great need arrived.

We had decided to file the lawsuit on July 20, the day we would leave for South Carolina to be present at my brother David's wedding. The critical period after filing the suit would likely be the first week the Robinsons received notice of it.

We planned to be absent from the West Side during the lawsuit's initial impact. Alberto would return home sometime around August 1. Joseph and I would remain in South Carolina until the fifteenth. Bernie would stay in our home for the week and a half we were all absent. He would also be there with Alberto while Joseph and I were in South Carolina. Bernie's presence with Alberto would be a relief. I did not want Alberto to be alone.

By the third week in July, Alberto and I were exhausted and anxious. We prayed that God would strengthen us for the days to come. Yet already God was calling the faithful to act on our behalf and accompany us on a journey we were too weak to take alone.

We received a phone call the weekend before our departure from Alberto's younger sister, Rebecca. Alberto has seven sisters. He is one of the oldest siblings in their family, and Rebecca one of the youngest. She was only five when Alberto left home to participate in A Better Chance program as a high school student in Minnesota. Rebecca graduated from high school in 1981; we had talked to her a few times about coming to Minnesota to attend college. She had been working during the year following her high school graduation, while living at home and caring for her parents.

When Rebecca spoke to Alberto, she referred to an urging of the Spirit similar to the experience that prompted Bernie to call us that summer.

"God has been speaking to me the last few weeks and telling me that you need me," Rebecca explained. "I've saved the money to fly out to Minnesota and I've made a reservation for August 17. If you tell me to come, I'll give notice, quit my job, and find work in St. Paul."

We assured Rebecca we did need her and finalized the details of her arrival. Afterward, I turned to Alberto joyfully and said, "The Lord will not let this house be empty. God will not let us be alone in this!" God would dwell with us through the faithful presence of Bernie and Rebecca in our home.

I did not understand all that was happening, but I knew it was providential. Many weeks later, Rebecca would tell me that, while still in California, she had disturbing dreams and visions. In her dreams, she could see large buildings. On August 17, as I drove her from the airport to our home, we passed by downtown St. Paul. The buildings in her dreams were shadows of the buildings of St. Paul. Her dreams also contained disturbing images of Alberto: in pain and in need. She would awake shaking, wanting to be with him.

Rebecca took her dreams seriously. She understood them as a way God spoke to her. She could have viewed the dreams as a premonition. Instead, she understood them as a calling—a call to get up and act on behalf of her brother. She responded to her dreams with faithfulness, embarking on a costly journey with us through the shadows of death. Her response was in the tradition of Ruth, the Moabitess, who long ago chose to accompany to Bethlehem one who called herself "Mara," which means *bitter*.

18

From the moment we awake until we fall asleep, we must commend our loved ones wholly and unreservedly to God, and leave them in His hands, transforming our anxiety for them into prayers on their behalf.
—Dietrich Bonhoeffer

Our trip to South Carolina in late July for my brother's wedding stirred mixed emotions. The wedding was a time of celebration. My family rejoiced over this marriage; it was a blessing to be included in the last-minute preparations and in the ceremony.

However, on our drive down to South Carolina and during the week of the wedding, I became increasingly concerned over Alberto's health. He had lost about 12 pounds. By the time we left for South Carolina, he weighed only 120. His clothes hung on him; his face was thin and lined with strain. His hair had taken on a silvery sheen, as if it might soon turn gray. He was becoming irritable, and at times quietly but frighteningly furious. Over the summer, he had become increasingly noncommunicative.

I sensed his constant tension. I had asked him repeatedly to see a doctor, but he never seemed to have the time. The distance between us was a gaping, treacherous hole in the fabric of our marriage.

On the way south, the tension erupted into a terrible scene. We were discussing our worrisome debt while driving through Lexington, Kentucky. Our monetary situation was a land mine of grievances. Alberto's practice was requiring more capital than the income it was producing, and I was worn out from holding two jobs and keeping our family budget.

Suddenly Alberto exploded. He was driving the car, and I begged him to pull over.

"I just can't go on any longer!" Alberto yelled. "You'll have to go to South Carolina without me. I'll put you and Joseph on a plane in Lexington, then head home by car."

"We can hardly afford two airline tickets," I pointed out icily.

We were both shouting at each other. Joseph began to cry. His cries stopped us both short. We took deep breaths. We agreed on a truce. We drove on but spoke as little as possible for the rest of the trip.

In South Carolina, Mom and Dad Wells tried to make our stay a restful one. I could read mounting concern in Mama's eyes.

One day we were sitting out on the porch together when she said, "I think I can learn to live with all the Robinsons took away from you and Alberto. But I couldn't bear for the loss to include your marriage."

That was the first time I had heard my thoughts voiced openly. I knew that in many ways Alberto and I were separated, living in the same household and sharing the same fears and protectiveness for our child. But we no longer shared joy or comfort. The partnership of our marriage was bleeding away, and I did not know how to staunch the wound.

Alberto left for Minnesota on August 1. I was thankful for Bernie's presence in our household, knowing that Alberto was not alone. I truly relaxed after Alberto left, taking with him the tension we could not ease between us. As usual, the time with my family passed all too quickly, and Joseph and I flew home.

Two days later, on August 17, Alberto's sister Rebecca arrived from California. Joseph and I went to the airport to meet her. I had not seen Rebecca in a year and a half. She brought with her joyful exuberance. I was happy to have her with us, and she seemed eager to begin a life in Minnesota with us.

The night following Rebecca's arrival, Alberto got up out of bed in the middle of the night and collapsed on the floor.

When I reached him, he was sweating profusely and was quite disoriented, muttering, "Where am I? Where am I?"

In those first few seconds, I felt certain he was having a heart attack. But before I could move to call the paramedics, he recovered. Rebecca and I discussed what we should do. I knew that during the few times Alberto had been ill since our marriage, his reactions to flus or viruses were often unusually severe.

I concluded that he must have a virus and had fainted from getting up too quickly. I put him to bed and watched over him awhile. Then I fell asleep. The next day, Alberto stayed home from the office. He seemed weak but said he felt fine.

That evening, as we were preparing for bed, I received a call from a member of the board of an alternative school for Native American youth in St. Paul—Red School House. I had applied for a part-time position there several months before. The woman who phoned explained that the school had a full-time teaching position available. Would I come in for an interview?

I hesitated. I explained I was interested in a part-time position because of my young child—but would be glad to come in for an interview. She scheduled an interview with the board of directors the next day.

About two hours after falling asleep, Alberto's frantic voice wakened me. "Helen, it's happening again!"

I ran in the direction of his voice, which was coming from the hallway leading to our bedroom. I found Alberto collapsed on the floor just as before. He was drenched in sweat and disoriented.

Rebecca came flying out of her room and stood beside us, very distressed. Again, Alberto's symptoms passed quickly, and Rebecca and I helped him back into bed. I told Alberto that I would definitely take him to a doctor the next day. He fell asleep immediately, and I lay beside him with my heart pounding.

The next morning, I called several general practitioners until I found one who would take us right away. Dr. DelaRosa's office had an afternoon appointment available. I went to my interview at Red School House and returned to pick up Alberto. After examining him, the doctor called for me. He would put Alberto in the hospital for tests. He told us to make arrangements for admission on Sunday afternoon. Tests would be done for hypoglycemia and for an ulcer on Monday.

The weekend passed quietly. I canned beans while Alberto rested. He slept off and on, while Joseph played contentedly by the couch where he lay. Rebecca helped me with canning and taking care of Alberto. Saturday afternoon Alberto came back from visiting our neighbors next door with a pair of crutches that they owned. He said he felt like he was going to fall down when he walked. I thought he was exaggerating.

Sunday afternoon, Alberto bathed before we left for the hospital. I stepped into the bathroom to bring him a towel. As I looked at him, fear gnawed at the edges of my mind. He looked suddenly gaunt, and his lips and gums seemed pale when he smiled. His hair looked silvery in the bathroom light.

I wondered if I was just upset and imagining all this. It seemed as if he was aging before my very eyes. I helped him dry off and dress. He kept repeating how tired he was. I was grateful that soon he would be able to rest completely in the hospital.

Rebecca stayed with Joseph while I took Alberto to the hospital. When we drove up to the admitting room, Alberto refused to walk in on his own.

He said over and over, "I'm just too tired to walk."

I felt exasperated. I was tired too, from constant stress and from caring for him the last few days—but I could still walk! I wished fervently that someone would check *me* into the hospital so I could sleep for a few days.

Finally I completed the admissions procedures, found a wheelchair, and got Alberto up to his room. In a few minutes, a nurse came in to take down some information.

After asking a few questions, she turned to me and said, "I know this sounds strange because your husband is dark-skinned, but does he seem pale to you?"

I was startled to hear my earlier observation of Alberto echoed by someone else. "Yes," I replied emphatically, "I noticed today that his lips and gums seem paler than usual."

The nurse turned back to Alberto. "You look as if you have been sick for some time, Mr. Quintela."

On Monday morning, I arrived back at the hospital early. I wanted to be there before they began the tests. When I entered Alberto's room, he was lying down, looking much worse than the day before. He had a heating pad on his head. His gums and lips were not just pale, they were white.

Alberto turned to me and explained that he had begun to experience a terrible headache in the night. He also said that they had taken a blood sample early in the morning and had canceled all the other scheduled tests until a doctor could arrive. Alberto said that his blood count was seriously low. Alberto's appearance and the words, "low blood count" sent me out of the room and to the nearest nurse for a fuller explanation. His nurse informed me that Alberto's hemoglobin, or red blood cell count, was 3.2.

"What's a normal hemoglobin level?" I asked.

"A normal count is 12 to 15 in men."

It seemed an eternity before Dr. DelaRosa got to the hospital. He explained that Alberto would need a blood transfusion soon. The intense headache Alberto was experiencing, as well as the fainting episodes at home and the extreme fatigue, were symptoms of insufficient oxygen.

However, medical personnel must complete blood tests before the initial transfusion could be administered. Once blood was given to Alberto, his true blood condition would be masked, making blood tests difficult. As we talked, the lab was running tests for sickle-cell anemia and other blood diseases. Dr. DelaRosa explained that he was bringing in a gastrointestinal specialist who would examine Alberto that morning.

The specialist, Dr. Lasser, arrived shortly afterward. His forcefulness filled the room. This was initially overwhelming, but as that long day wore on, I came to greatly appreciate this physician who remained late into the night, determined to reach a diagnosis before Alberto became weaker.

Dr. Lasser's examination revealed that Alberto had blood in his stool, indicating internal bleeding. Dr. Lasser said the bleeding was probably occurring in the stomach or in the small intestine. He was puzzled, however, that Alberto had not experienced any abdominal pain. He told us he would order a complete set of gastrointestinal x-rays. He was looking for a bleeding ulcer. The amount of internal bleeding that Alberto had experienced was extreme, indicating he might have a perforated stomach or intestine. A perforation would require surgery.

X-rays did not indicate an ulcer. All the blood tests were negative. By late evening, we seemed no closer to a diagnosis. Both Dr. Lasser and Dr. DelaRosa seemed worried and tense. I knew without asking that we were facing the possibility of cancer. Alberto was physically exhausted and emotionally depleted as the day ended.

I left the hospital that evening feeling absolutely

numb. I went home to Rebecca and Joseph. After talking on the phone to my parents, who sounded as concerned as I was, I prepared to sleep.

I took Joseph in my arms and carried him with me to my bedroom. Joseph was frantic and so hyperactive I didn't know how I would ever get him to sleep or where I would find the strength to calm him. I lay down with him, and Rebecca came into the room to tell us good-night. I looked into her eyes and saw my own fear and uncertainty mirrored there.

"Would you sleep here with us?" I asked.

"I think we need to pray," Rebecca said quietly, lying down and hugging Joseph to her.

The three of us lay there and Rebecca prayed aloud for us. As she prayed, I could sense Joseph relaxing and falling asleep in her arms. Her prayer was a bond between us and God. She had reached out and taken God's hand on behalf of us all.

Long after she slept, I lay in the dark, eyes wide open, talking to the One from whom I had turned my face for several months. I asked God how we would ever face a diagnosis of cancer. "Dear God," I cried out wordlessly, "Is this the way I'm to lose Alberto?"

19

Let all who take refuge in you be glad;
let them ever sing for joy.
Spread your protection over them,
that those who love your name may rejoice in you.
—Psalm 5:11

I returned to the hospital early Tuesday morning. As I walked down the hall toward Alberto's room, I spotted him lying on a stretcher near the elevator. I was stunned to see how thin and weak he appeared, as if he had lost ground overnight.

He seemed barely conscious. The nurses said that his headache, which had improved after Monday's transfusions, had returned. They were now taking Alberto to another part of the hospital for a *gastroscopy*. The internal surface of the stomach would be examined through a special instrument passed through the mouth and down the esophagus. Dr. Lasser would perform the procedure. I could accompany Alberto.

When we were left in the examining room alone, Alberto turned to me and spoke weakly, but forcefully. "I'm not going to sign a permission for the test. They said it requires anesthesia, and I won't let them put me out, not with this headache. I feel like I might never wake up."

I sensed in Alberto the same fears that churned inside of me. I said gently, "Alberto, we have to know what is wrong. It may be something that can be healed. We have to at least know what we're facing."

"I won't sign any papers," he repeated, and closed his eyes.

I waited for Dr. Lasser. When he arrived, he explained the procedure to us. Alberto would be given a drug to relax his muscles so a tube could be inserted down the esophagus and into the stomach. He would be awake, but very relaxed. Dr. Lasser would be able to see the stomach lining through the scope. He would look for an ulcer. If he failed to see one, he would take a small amount of tissue for a biopsy.

When Dr. Lasser presented the release paper for the procedure, Albert made no move to take it. "I'll sign it," I said. "Alberto, I am going to sign this with your permission. We have to know what is wrong."

Alberto nodded weakly. I signed the permission. The nurse showed me where I could wait.

I did not have to wait long. Dr. Lasser came bounding through the door of the examining room, a big smile on his usually stern face.

"It's an ulcer!" he exclaimed. "I know that may not seem like good news to you, but you know, I was afraid he might have cancer."

I knew. And I too felt immeasurably grateful.

"We'll begin more blood transfusions and medication right away," Dr. Lasser explained. "He'll feel better soon. The ulcer is surprisingly small and is not perforated. He'll be fine!"

From that day, our lives changed again, but this time, it was with a sense of blessing and promise. Brushing against death, we had seen life more clearly. Both Alberto and I had lived for the year since the fire with haunting questions about the worth of our lives.

We had doubted that we would find the strength to go on living and the value of even trying. Likewise we had questioned the worth of our marriage. Our marriage had been bleeding to death just as surely as Alberto had been bleeding. We had not known how to keep life from pouring out of our union with one another. Our grasp on life was as tentative as the reach of the woman who came up behind Jesus, touching the hem of his cloak.

Yet God sees even our most hesitant longing to be healed and to live. "Daughter, your faith has healed you. Go in peace."

Even the action of one who can only summon the desire to reach out in mute longing is blessed as faithfulness. God holds nothing back from us. Our lives are pure gift. Even when our lives are crushed by brokenness and despair, they are still precious to God. God does not distinguish between a life that is fruitful and a life that is crushed. Surely the resurrection of one condemned and broken on the cross is witness to God's everlasting concern that we live, and live abundantly.

After those days in the hospital, when Alberto came home, our lives took on meaning again. We had the gift of Alberto's life, and we prepared to live out of the promise of that gift. Dr. Lasser had told Alberto that he would need to rest for several months. Alberto was determined to follow the doctor's instructions so he could regain his health.

He gave me the information I would need to close down his law practice. The board of directors at Red School House offered me a full-time position as reading coordinator and instructor. I accepted. Rebecca arranged to work for a local dentist in the afternoons and evenings. Thus she could care for Joseph in the mornings, leaving him in Alberto's care for his afternoon nap hours. I would be home soon after Joseph woke up each day so that Alberto's responsibilities would be lightened for the fall.

Those autumn days were filled with a light that began to lead us out of darkness. On the days that Rebecca did not work in the afternoons, I would stay at school a little later, preparing for the next day. I remember coming home near dinnertime, stepping into the kitchen where she would be making supper with Joseph playing at her feet.

For the first time in two and a half years, I looked forward to coming home. I could not wait to come through the door and see the faces of those I loved. I longed to hear them tell the precious details of their day.

Near Christmas, Rebecca asked if she could decorate the house. I didn't answer right away. Decorating the house would mean opening the box of ornaments and decorations that had been preserved from the fire.

On the first Christmas following the fire, I had opened the box and detected a faint smell of smoke. I had closed the box back up and decided not to put anything out for Christmas. Joseph was toddling around and I reasoned that he would only pull a tree over on himself anyway. But this Christmas my parents were coming, and Rebecca wanted to prepare the house. I gave her the box.

As the days turned snowy and cold, I began to anticipate my parent's visit. School closed for Christmas vacation. Joseph was excited and alive with curiosity over all the celebrative occasions of the season. Alberto looked well. He had received a job offer from the Minnesota state department of commerce and would begin in January. Our financial situation was slowly righting itself, and when Alberto went back to work we could begin to pay off debts.

My parents arrived. On Christmas eve, we all piled in our car to drive to Faith Mennonite Church. Since most people in the congregation have family in rural communities several hours from the cities, few people were left in the city to celebrate Christmas together. Yet these were always some of my favorite gatherings. I was drawn closer to the sisters and brothers that were there, as if our being left together signified more fully our relationship in Jesus Christ.

On that Christmas eve, one member, Frank Trnka, had planned the service. He had pulled chairs together in a circle around a table with a single candle burning in a large holder. The lights were dimmed, and the faces of each person glowed softly in the muted light of the candle's flame.

At one point, Frank asked each of us to consider a gift that we might give to God that evening. He asked us to write down our gifts on small pieces of paper, and then to offer them up through the flame of the candle.

In the prayer ceremonies at Red School House,

where I had been teaching, we always offered our prayers to the Creator through sage dropped into the flames of a small fire. The sweet-smelling smoke rose up out of the flames, just as our prayers rose up to God. Frank's imagery, of letting our promises to God be released from the papers and rise up to the Creator, was very meaningful to me.

As I sat there, time suddenly seemed to stand still. Everyone else's face seemed to recede. The great quietness of the past July night on my porch stole over me again. Only this time, in the stillness, I could hear my own heart pounding.

There was one thing that I had withheld from God—one decision I had made as a curse upon the life that God had given me. I had decided there would be no more children for us. I had decided I didn't want—didn't need—any more gifts of life from the hands of the Creator. I looked down at the small white piece of paper, and thought of putting it into the flame blank. I knew I could easily promise anything else. But I also knew that any other promise would not unlock my control over what I would do with my life.

In this matter, the Great Healer awaited that hesitant reaching out for the hem of his cloak. For to reach out and take hold of the cloak, one must release whatever is being gripped so tightly in one's hand.

And so it was that I opened my hand. I took up a pencil, wrote the words of a promise, and slipped them into the fire.

20

And his name was Daniel, which means, "God is my judge."

On November 7, 1983, our son Daniel was born. He was born three weeks before he was expected. Many medical personnel had gathered to deliver this premature infant. Yet when my doctor lifted him out of the womb and held him up, he let out a lusty cry that reflected his strong, fully mature, seven-pound body. The whole room filled with the smiles and laughter of relief. We had all miscalculated!

My mother arrived hurriedly on a plane that morning. She brought Joseph to see his brother late in the afternoon. Joseph looked with astonishment at this little bundle of waving arms and legs. All our careful preparations could not quite match the reality of this little one who had been given into our family. Joseph leaned way over the bassinet to plant a kiss on Daniel's mouth. He seemed satisfied that the baby belonged in some special way to him.

But no joy over the baby's birth could match Alberto's. He sat for hours holding the baby, talking to him, weaving bonds between father and child. During those days and in the weeks to come, Alberto's face began to take on shades of peace and celebration.

The winter passed swiftly. It was an unusually cold and snowy year. At home with Joseph and Daniel, I relaxed contentedly into caring for them both. Daniel slept much of the day during his first few months. Joseph and I filled the days with reading, painting, playing, and listening to music. Joseph loved to have little friends over to our house, and so we often had another child to share our days.

Alberto had been serving for several years in a consulting position with the Hispanic Ministries program for the General Conference Mennonite Church. Alberto was also interested in developing a Mennonite witness and presence on the West Side of St. Paul. He felt that the Mennonite Church, with its strong family values—resembling the extended family values of the Hispanic community—could witness to Hispanic persons concerned about justice and peace.

During the summer before Daniel was born, we had asked that a Hispanic ministerial intern come to the West Side. The intern would hold summer seminars on peace and justice issues and continue a Spanish radio program that Alberto had started. The radio program addressed such issues as family violence, community relationships, and concerns of refugees from Central and South America.

In the summer of 1983, the General Conference sent Marco Guete and his family to St. Paul for a summer internship. Marco had graduated from the Hispanic Ministries program at Goshen College. He was on his way to Chicago in September to begin seminary and start a church among the Hispanic community there.

Marco brought along a young man who had graduated from Goshen's Hispanic Ministries program and had worked for a time in California. Apolinar Nava wanted to help start a Bible study fellowship on the West Side. During the summer, he helped Marco visit homes in our community and also helped with the weekly Spanish radio programs.

When it was time for Marco and his family to leave for Chicago, Apolinar decided to remain in St. Paul. He felt he had the nucleus for a small Spanish-speaking Bible study group on the West Side.

During the winter Daniel was born, and into the spring, Apolinar met weekly with a group of 20-30 people for singing, prayer, and Bible study. His outgoing nature made it easy for him to invite people to visit the growing group. But the harsh winter environment was a great hardship for Apolinar, who was accustomed to warmer climates. He confided to Alberto in April that he wanted to leave Minnesota and return to his family in Mexico.

Alberto quickly tried to find someone who could come and continue Apolinar's important work. We had begun to receive regular mission funds from the Northern District of the General Conference to finance Apolinar's part-time position. Alberto wrote to Goshen College, asking whether a graduate from the Hispanic Ministries program could come to St. Paul. But Spanish-speaking church workers were in great demand, and the program's two graduates that year were already committed elsewhere.

I had attended few of the fellowship meetings in St. Paul, because I spoke little Spanish and the winter was too harsh for taking the baby and Joseph out in the cold. Yet I sensed Alberto's deep disappointment that the group would be leaderless. He did not feel he had the time or the gifts to be the leader.

Apolinar left. As Alberto had anticipated, the group fell apart. Yet we still had the mission funds available if we could find a church worker.

One night in May, Alberto and I were lying in bed after the children were asleep, talking about the church work on the West Side.

"I've been wanting to ask you something," Alberto said. "I don't want you to answer at first, but to think about what I'm going to suggest. I want to ask if you would lead the fellowship until we can find another worker. You're a gifted teacher. You could teach the Bible and lead prayer and singing.

"I know it would have to be primarily an English-speaking group. We'd have to begin a new group anyway because Apolinar's group has already fallen apart. Besides, most families on the West Side are English-speaking. They are second and even third-generation residents.

"I want us to preserve a Mennonite witness in some form on the West Side. If you're willing, we'll go to the mission board in June and ask them if you could take Apolinar's position."

Like Sarah, when she heard the angel say that she would bear a son in her old age, I almost laughed aloud. But something stopped the laughter even as it bubbled up. As I gazed at Alberto's face, I knew how much this witness meant to him. I decided that I would consider the position, if only for the hope it gave to him.

During the next few days, I had many running arguments with God. I reminded the One who made me that I had taken only one biblical course in all my years of schooling. I reminded God how little contentment and peace I had been allowed in the past four years. I told God to go find someone else.

Finally I said I would do it until next spring, but if someone else didn't show up by then, it would be in God's hands, not on mine. I was going back to teaching.

I told Alberto I would lead the fellowship until next spring. I went with him to the Northern District conference in June. With the support of the home missions committee, Alberto and I returned to St. Paul and set an early August date for the first fellowship meeting.

We would begin by visiting the homes of people who had attended Apolinar's group, inviting them to participate in the newly organized fellowship. We also planned to ask Faith Church members for their support. Since the group would be in English, some members might even be willing to regularly attend the fellowship meetings.

An Advisory Council to supervise the new work at the St. Paul Mennonite Fellowship was organized on June 25. It was made up of Faith Mennonite Church members as well as Pastor Myron Schrag.

Meanwhile, Alberto's sister Rebecca was planning to be married on August 5. My mother and father-in-law would make their first trip to Minnesota for her wedding. I threw myself into helping her make wedding plans, and the summer flew by.

She and her husband, Steven Smith, would continue to live in St. Paul while she finished at the College of St. Catherine's. I was glad she would not be far away. I had come to depend on her constant love and support.

On August 14, we prepared for our first fellowship meeting, in the dining room of our home. Three people were present—myself, Alberto, and a young woman from Faith Church, Terry Gerber. The three of us sat around my grandmother's old oak dining table, encouraging one another. We prayed that God would make this little group of three into a viable witness on St. Paul's West Side.

Three nights later, on a Saturday evening, we had a potluck in our backyard, to which we invited all who were interested in the vision. A large group of about 50 showed up. They included people from Faith church, people from the community who had participated in Apolinar's study group, and friends and neighbors.

We had arranged to have a mariachi band from a Mexican orphanage play for the group after the meal. The band was composed of children and young people of all ages, and was in the United States raising money for their orphanage. It was a delightful evening and greatly encouraged us as we began the long hard task of planting a Mennonite church group on the West Side.

In September, I enrolled in a New Testament course with Professor Henry Gustafson at United Theological Seminary of the Twin Cities. I had decided I couldn't lead this group for even a few months without some sort of biblical course for myself. Alberto found a family willing to care for Joseph and Daniel on the day I would attend seminary.

I traveled the waters of a new river that year, from September to May, moving hesitantly through unknown channels. Yet these uncharted channels were streams of grace. Henry's class in New Testament began to intrigue me, and then to challenge all the ways I had ever understood Scripture.

Suddenly the biblical witness came alive, speaking in a tongue I had never heard. I could not put it down. I read all year with the excitement that I remembered had always characterized my mother's encounters with Scripture.

Throughout the autumn and early winter months, we held fellowship meetings in our home or in the home of one of the former participants in the Spanish-speaking Bible study.

Another young woman from Faith Church, Karen Wiebe, joined us regularly. She played guitar, and so on the nights she was with us, we had hymn-sing. Besides hymn-sing, we regularly shared our praises and concerns with one another, prayed, and studied a Scripture passage.

In January, Alberto organized a door-to-door invitational. He wanted to introduce our new fellowship group to the West Side community. We would invite anyone to attend a 12-week Bible study, to be held Wednesday nights at Neighborhood House, a local community center.

He asked Faith Church members to help us with the door-to-door invitational each Saturday morning in

January. Most of us thought such a visitation in the middle of a Minnesota winter was crazy. We teased Alberto about it, but most of our banter was to cover up our hesitancy to go out and knock on the doors of our neighbors. What if they slammed the door?

Because of our hesitancy, Alberto carefully organized the experience for us. The folks who were participating met together for a meal each Saturday morning. Alberto and I prepared a filling Mexican breakfast and plenty of coffee. After breakfast, we had a time of prayer and encouragement.

Then we started out on our assigned streets. Alberto sent us out in teams of two, with booklets in which to record responses. He had given us questions to ask if people were willing to spend a few minutes with us.

The first question was whether persons already attended a church regularly. If not, we asked if they would like information about our fellowship. If they were interested, we described our young group and invited them to attend the Bible study.

When the teams came back after about two or three hours, we gathered to tell of our encounters. These sharing times were exuberant. We were all doing something we never thought we could. We felt especially blessed when we met other Christians who assured us they would pray for us and our efforts.

We were blessed with some unexpected results from the four Saturdays of knocking on doors. Although no one new showed up for the first Wednesday night Bible study, two people from Faith Church decided to support us by attending.

Thus we had a core group of six people from the

"mother church." They included Alberto, myself, Terry, Karen, and now Warren Fuller and John Tiessen. By late spring, two women from the community had read about us in the West Side newspaper and began to attend. Two other men from the Faith Church community, Larry Mellom and Thomas Yousey, also began to attend regularly.

May began. We had a core group now of eight, with two others from the community who attended regularly. Earlier, I had told God that this was where I was turning back. I had only agreed to give it nine months. I had told God to find someone else to come and take up the work in St. Paul.

No one else came. God had found someone. Whenever I looked in the mirror, I laughed like Sarah. But whenever I looked at the little fellowship group, I did not laugh. Out of the ashes of my despair, God was giving birth to a people.

EPILOGUE: THE ST. PAUL MENNONITE FELLOWSHIP TODAY

For you, O Lord, have delivered my soul from death,
my eyes from tears,
my feet from stumbling,
that I may walk before the Lord in the land of the living.
                    —Psalm 116

The St. Paul Mennonite Fellowship, located on the West Side of St. Paul, celebrated its sixth anniversary in August 1990. The fellowship stands within the Anabaptist tradition out of which the Mennonite Church grew. It is strongly evangelical in its consistently articulated invitation to others to participate in the fellowship of faith.

This "invitation to faith" through the community of God's gathered people is at the heart of the fellowship's understanding of the gospel message. The community of faith (the church) is closely identified with the body of Christ, ministering in and for the world.

The fellowship is strongly committed to peace and

justice issues, especially those that arise from the family and community context. Thus there is a concern about domestic violence, discrimination against the poor, racial discrimination and its resulting violence, and refugee needs.

The fellowship follows the Anabaptist pattern of strong congregational authority, of scriptural interpretation and discernment by the gathered body, and a dependence on the guidance and empowerment of the Holy Spirit.

However, while the fellowship stands strongly within the Anabaptist context, it certainly belongs to the prophetic, or renewal, edge of the Mennonite Church. The fellowship is a "new thing" which has been called into being in the Mennonite Church. It models an alternative form of congregational life within a tradition in crisis because of the passing away of traditional patterns centered around farming.

Worldwide, the Mennonite Church is rapidly becoming an urban, multiethnic, multilingual denomination. It is being called out of a long period of isolation and separation from "the world." Such emergence is painful but necessary, and there are new bonds of partnership being forged between "old" and "new" Mennonites. The St. Paul fellowship is itself financially supported by many rural churches or church groups, as well as by home missions committees of two districts.

The life of the St. Paul Mennonite Fellowship is best understood as a family. Members are reborn into family-type relationships with God and with one another through Jesus Christ. The fellowship takes seriously the proclamation of Jesus of Nazareth that "here are my mother and my sisters and my brothers."

Many of the fellowship members are far from extended family. Some have come out of dysfunctional family settings. The community of faith has truly become family. In fact, the community often greets visitors with a song, "God's Family," which is the childrens' favorite song. The song articulates the fellowship's understanding of its life together. It also reminds members that this family is open, always expecting the "birth" of new family members.

Thus the fellowship has taken the Anabaptist heritage of strong familial ties, often used as a model for the family of God, and turned that model upside down. Instead of taking the human family system as model for the family of God, the fellowship sees the family of God as model for the human family.

The fellowship articulates the hope of faith to those members for whom the human family has been a tragic and/or abusive environment. The community envisions a new family—given new life and a future of peace through the Spirit of one who became our brother, reconciling us to God, our Parent.

The fellowship's understanding of table fellowship and hospitality is consistent with this understanding of its life as family in Christ. In its earliest years, the fellowship met first around our dining room table, and later around a table at the local community center. As we have grown too large for gathering around a table, the fellowship has adopted a circular arrangement of chairs for worship, study and prayer, and consensus meetings.

Because some who come to fellowship are literally hungry, food is shared at almost every gathering. Homes of fellowship members are usually open to unexpected visitors for meals. The fellowship sees hospitality and table fellowship as integral parts of the gospel message. The fellowship remembers that Jesus of Nazareth ate with those to whom he ministered. He shared the blessings and the nourishment of table fellowship with those cast out or ostracized from this healing circle of fellowship and love.

The St. Paul Mennonite Fellowship could appropriately be described as an evangelical fellowship. Its presence in an urban community of diverse peoples is rooted in the sharing of the gospel's good news of being one people reconciled to our Creator.

Evangelism is a call to table fellowship, an invitation to the table of the Lord. The evangelist is one who shares the good news of God's everlasting love through ministry to those in need, comforting those burdened with grief or despair, and becoming sister or brother to another by invitation to a common table. Conversion means the conversion of the evangelist to the side of one cast out, alone, or hurting. Thus we expect our own conversion when we sit down at the table with the one who has been invited there.

A good example of this understanding of evangelism and evangelist is the two door-to-door invitationals which fellowship members participated in during the first two years of the fellowship.

In the winter of both 1985 and 1986, many of us went door-to-door on the West Side, meeting our neighbors and inviting them to prayer meeting and Bible study. Out of these efforts, during which we contacted about 200 homes, one person actually joined the fellowship.

However, the invitationals were also the beginning of our own conversion to the West Side community. Through the experience, we learned to know and trust "the folks." We came to know our community in a way that looked at it, not past it.

Two years ago, the fellowship invited a unit of eight Mennonite Voluntary Service workers to join with us on the West Side. They each worked in agencies that provide services to persons in the West Side community. The continued presence of voluntary service workers today is a witness to the one present through and among us in our urban neighborhood.

The St. Paul fellowship is also shaped by the experiences of exile and oppression shared by some of its minority members. Early in the life of the fellowship, the group helped to sponsor a young man from El Salvador, who came to live with our family. He was the first person to join the fellowship who spoke only Spanish. His presence affirmed our vision to become a multiethnic (perhaps, one day, bilingual) community.

Our Hispanic adult members and our children who are ethnically diverse remind us of the sojourner in the land. Many of our members feel estranged from the dominant culture, which views them as "foreigners." For some, their uncertain legal status accentuates this self-image as the "alien."

This self-understanding is very much akin to the self-understanding of many traditional Mennonite communities. The Mennonite self-understanding is expressed in the phrase, "being in the world, yet not of the world." There is an understanding of belonging to a kingdom that is of God, while sojourning in the kingdom of this world.

This understanding can cause isolation and a loss of witness to the world. It can also, however, result in a sense of prophetic tension with the dominant culture and a solidarity with those who feel like strangers—sojourners—in their own land.

My leadership as church planter and pastor of the St. Paul Mennonite Fellowship has been a growth into ministry as the group itself has matured. I have traveled these streams of grace for six years now, not always certain of where they are leading me, but growing more confident that their source is the Creator of all wisdom.

Our civil lawsuit, filed in July 1982, was finally settled in an out-of-court agreement in December 1986. As time wore on and the legal process unfolded, Alberto and I lost heart for a face-to-face confrontation with the disturbed Robinson family.

Time itself was a factor in this reluctance. After four years, the wounds of our experience were beginning to heal in the context of our church community and the growing fellowship on the West Side. We were hesitant to enter a situation that might reopen our wounds. Our focus had already shifted to learning to live on with the scars we bear. The fellowship had been planted and was thriving. We did not want to turn our energy away from its life-giving growth.

The first few years of any church planting effort are risky ones. The gifts God calls out when a new congregation is born are much like gifts the parent of an infant must exercise. The founding pastor must nurture and protect, love and encourage a strong self-identity in the young church, tell and retell the story of the church's birth and growth, and look forward to its future in the hands of the Creator. The personal investment is enormous; so are the joys and the burdens.

There comes a time when the body has matured enough to assert some independence. The independence of the St. Paul Mennonite Fellowship was celebrated on September 11, 1988. That day we gathered with our parent congregation, Faith Mennonite, to be commissioned as a "sister" congregation and to begin our own Sunday worship times. It was a day of sorrow and gladness, during which we received the blessings of the parent congregation, who nurtured us throughout the years of our "infancy."

I have had to make the transition from founding pastor to pastor—from pastor of an infant congregation to a maturing, independent body. This has happened slowly, but with the same mixture of joy and sorrow present in the September 11 commissioning.

One day, during a particularly painful time, I was preparing the story of the wedding at Cana for the children of the fellowship. In that story I heard something I had never heard before. This day, on which Jesus began his ministry, was a day Jesus himself did not anticipate.

According to the story, Jesus is caught by surprise over his mother's request. He knows he must embark on God's ministry among his people, but he wrestles with the timing. God uses his mother, Mary of Nazareth, to reveal that the time is at hand. She knows he is ready. She has faith in his God-given powers.

"Do whatever he tells you to do," she says.

Mary of Nazareth has pondered many things. She surely understands that this day marks the beginning of Jesus' ministry, but also the end of her time for protection and nurture of him. She is sending him out—to pain and sacrifice that will finally envelop her as well.

In this story, Mary reveals a mother's love transformed. She moves with grace to that stage of parenting in which we must let go of our children, believing God's love will be with them in ways we can no longer be.

It is like the day that I put Joseph on the bus for his first day of kindergarten. Until that day, I had nurtured him and protected him as best I could. I had loved him fiercely and taught him all I felt he needed to know to grow up into this day.

But standing on the curb and watching that bus leave with him hurt! I knew I could no longer stand between him and the world—a world that at best is intolerant of people who are different. I knew that from that day on, my role would be to help him integrate what we as his parents had taught him (and would teach him) with what the world would show him.

As the fellowship matures, I've felt that I'm standing on that street corner, watching the fellowship move into a stage of life which calls for a transformation in my pastoral care. The gifts God called out in me the first few years are now being called out in others, creating a priesthood of all believers in the life of the fellowship. I am being called to a trust in God and in my brothers and sisters that recognizes their faithfulness and love for the body I have loved so deeply.

As I participate in the life of this young congregation, I feel privileged to have helped and witnessed its birth, to have been its midwife.

Yet, when, exactly did the birth occur? The night Alberto turned to me six years ago and asked if I would prepare for and commit myself to the journey he so strongly envisioned?

Or was it the night, five-and-a-half years ago, that Alberto, I, and Terry Gerber gathered around our dining room table, and with doubts and with faith, started the journey to which God would add more and more travelers, big and small?

Was it the night six of us gathered for a potluck meal to which we had invited and hoped for many others— suddenly realizing *we* were the ones invited to a meal already prepared by the host?

Or does the birth even go back to the day I held our son Daniel in my arms and acknowledged that God does truly desire life for us, even after we have traveled in the shadows of death and tragedy and destruction?

Perhaps the prophet Hosea proclaimed that moment most eloquently:

> I will plant her for myself in the land;
> I will show my love to the one I called "Not my loved
>   one."
> I will say to those called "Not my people," "You are my
>   people;"
> and they will say, "You are my God."

BIBLIOGRAPHY

Burns, Olive Ann. *Cold Sassy Tree*. New York: Dell Publishing Co., 1984.

Davis, Stephen T., ed. *Encountering Evil: Live Options in Theodicy*. Atlanta: John Knox Press, 1973.

Gustafson, Henry. "The Afflictions of Christ: What Is Lacking?" *Biblical Research VIII* (1963): 28-42.

Hall, Douglas John. *Lighten Our Darkness: Toward an Indigenous Theology of the Cross*. Philadelphia: The Westminster Press, 1976.

Hallie, Philip. *Lest Innocent Blood Be Shed*. New York: Harper & Row, 1979.

Kushner, Harold S. *When Bad Things Happen to Good People*. New York: Schocken Books, 1981.

Niebuhr, Reinhold. *The Nature and Destiny of Man*. New York: Scribners, 1949.

Sider, Ronald J. *Christ and Violence*. Scottdale: Herald Press, 1979.

Soelle, Dorothee. *Suffering*. Translated by Everett R. Kalin. Philadelphia: Fortress Press, 1973.

Vieth, Richard F. *Holy Power, Human Pain*. Bloomington: Meyer Stone Books, 1988.

Yoder, John H. *Christian Attitudes to War, Peace, and Revolution*. Elkhart: Distibuted by Co-op Bookstore, 1983.

Yoder, John H. *Nevertheless: A Meditation on the Varieties and Shortcomings of Religious Pacifism*. Scottdale: Herald Press, 1971.

THE AUTHOR

Helen Quintela (right) with Alberto and sons Daniel (left) and Joseph.

Helen Wells Quintela grew up in Greenville, South Carolina, where her family was active in the Methodist church. Following graduation from Queens College

(Charlotte, N.C.), she attended Harvard University's Graduate School of Education. There she met her husband, Alberto Quintela, Jr. The first thing she and Albert shared was a terrible case of homesickness!

After completing their degrees in 1976, Helen and Alberto settled in Minneapolis, Minnesota. Helen taught fifth grade in the Chaska (Minn.) public schools until 1980. As a graduate student and as a teacher she had a special interest in reading disabilities.

Shortly before the birth of their oldest child, Helen and Alberto moved to an urban neighborhood of St. Paul (Minn.). *Out of Ashes* tells of their struggle to make this neighborhood home for their family of mixed color and ethnic backgrounds.

Helen is founding pastor of the St. Paul Mennonite Fellowship, begun in 1984. This urban, Anabaptist congregation dreams that one day many peoples will become God's people, celebrating differences and working for family, community, and world peace. Sharing that vision, Helen, Alberto, and their sons Joseph and Daniel live today in urban St. Paul.